HOMEGROWN

ON THE

FARM

HONED BY LIFE

AND

BLESSED OF GOD

EUNICE PADGETT

ISBN 978-1-0980-3050-6 (paperback)
ISBN 978-1-0980-3051-3 (digital)

Christian Faith Publishing, Inc.
832 Park Avenue
Meadville, PA 16335
www.christianfaithpublishing.com

Unless otherwise indicated, all scripture quotations are from the King James Version of the Bible.

Front Cover Photography—Nate Nimocks
Cover Artwork—Mark Risley
Back cover insert photography—Andrea Hall

Printed in the United States of America

Memorial Dedication

This book is dedicated to the memory of John William Adkison and Bessie Mae Rushing Adkison. They were the best parents for which a girl could ask. I consider myself blessed to have been theirs. They taught me how to live life and enjoy the journey. They showed me by example that God was with me through the good and the bad. Daddy taught me to stand tall, head held high, shoulders back, and to have a song in my heart. Mama taught me to love people, look for the best in any situation, and give space for healing and correction. They both showed me by example how to embrace a life lived for God. I am forever indebted to them for the good, loving, sturdy, and righteous foundation upon which to build a life and a legacy. Thank you, Mama and Daddy. I will always cherish our years together.

Eunice Adkison Padgett (2013)

Except the Lord build the house,
they labor in vain that build it...

—Psalm 127:1

CONTENTS

ACKNOWLEDGMENTS
AND DEDICATIONS

*B*ooks are never written alone.

First and foremost, I am thankful to my Lord and Savior Jesus Christ. He is the Anchor of my soul. He is the Giver of hope. He is my Strength and Guide for this journey called Life. He is my Everything. Always.

I give thanks to my mother and father. Their example taught me not only how to live, but how to die. I am forever grateful for the pattern of love and the Godly principles they established for me to follow.

To my husband, John, I give honor, love, and thanks. You are the dearest thing in my life. You willingly took over when Mama and Daddy said, "She's yours." You did Daddy such a favor! You have helped me implement and intertwine the principles found in this book into daily living. You encouraged me as I took my writings and scribbled thoughts and put them into printed book form. I would never have gotten it accomplished without your encouragement and support. It has been a privilege and a blessing to have you by my side these almost fifty years. You have satisfied me well and made my life full, pleasing, and fun. I love you and am honored to be your wife. I not only dedicate this book to you, but my life.

Along with my parents and husband, I dedicate this book to my precious children, Greg and Melissa. You have allowed me to use your names in storytelling many times; I have tried to not present embarrassing moments. You both have kept me on my toes and knees but look what a great mom that has made me (*smile*).

I know no greater joy than that you "walk in truth" and have placed your lives in the hands of the Author of Life. I love you both with all my heart. You have made me proud to be called your mother.

Kimberly, my daughter-in-law and gift from God, you are lovely inside and out. Thanks for loving my son. I love you.

And, Nate, the son-in-law God gave us to make our daughter's heart smile. Nate, I love you and I love the way you love God.

I also dedicate this book to my four awesome grandchildren. Joel, Daniel, Gabriel, and Anna, I love you to the moon a hundred, thousand, million, trillion, gazillion times, and back. My prayer is you, too, will embrace Godly life principles and live for Him with all your heart.

With love, I give honor and thanks to my siblings. Each of you has contributed so much to my life. The times enjoyed together "on the farm" are cherished memories. I am blessed that we are family.

Thanks to the individuals of New Life Pentecostal Church. You have loved me through the learning, leanness, and sorrow. You shared my joy in the bountiful and pleasant times. It has been an honor to serve you alongside my husband through the years. You have been the recipient of the life lessons learned "from the farm" because of my role as your pastor's wife. You are the best. I love you dearly.

DECLARATION

*N*o work in print has been accomplished by only one person. We are each presented with ideas all through life. Our thoughts, opinions, and views are influenced by our parents, teachers, family, and others with whom we come in contact. Words spoken, things we see and hear, and what we read cause a thought process to develop in our own minds. It does us well to pass these thoughts through the filter of the Holy Scripture. We must ask questions, "Is this right? Is this wrong? Is this Truth? Is this what I want influencing my thoughts?" We cannot embrace them as our own until they have been refined and aligned with God's Word. It is only then we dare allow these ideas, words, and views to become a resource for an approach to express and communicate our deepest feelings whether written or spoken.

I have been an enthusiastic reader and note "jotter" all my life. Yet carefulness to write down the origination of a comment or statement read or heard was often neglected. Many of my notes are several years old going back to my teenage years and I have long since forgotten the source that prompted some of my thought process and "just thinking." With regret, after a diligent search, it was impossible to locate the original source whether it is a book, article, radio program, or preached message from which these were read or heard. Consequently, I am unable to give credit to the originator of some statements included in this book. If you find that I have quoted something you may have read in another publication or source, for that I apologize. It is never my intention to plagiarize and no intentional reproduction of content is intended.

INTRODUCTION

*I*f you were to read my daily journals, hopefully you would feel the depth of my feelings, thoughts, and emotions. I pull these journals out of storage from time to time and reflect on the events of my life. Being reminded of the blessings and the victories God has given me is reassuring.

Opening the heart, whether it be written or spoken, makes one vulnerable to criticism and misunderstanding. My hope is that while reading, you are given insight to who I am; a girl with a big heart, full of love for life and laughter, and an appreciation for God, family, and friends.

Through the years, I have written many of my thoughts about family. Some of them have been in the form of letters. Most, however, have been recorded in my journal as life lessons that Mama and Daddy taught me. They are precious memories of days gone by.

When Mama became so sick, I began asking questions and collecting information that might have otherwise been lost to me. I regret not asking questions sooner, getting additional facts and documenting the information in more detail.

In 2013–2014 I spent much time "on the farm" with Daddy, asking him about life and reflecting on my childhood. This has been a time of bittersweet memories and a reminder of how blessed I was and am.

As Daddy's ninety-ninth birthday was nearing he told me, *"My birthday is getting close and I don't need anything for the house, and I have enough clothes to last me until I die. If y'all want to do something for me just write a memory on a card, letter, scrap of paper or a book."*

I diligently set out to compile my jotted thoughts for him. I dug out some of my old writings and added new; the result is this book.

As I presented Daddy the notes, cards, and letters the day of his birthday party, I told him that I had written him a book. He replied, *"I kind of thought you would."* He knew all the questions, writing and recorded interviews were for a purpose. I am thankful I could read a few pages of the script to him, although it was through tears from both of us.

I hope as you read these pages you can find yourself on "the farm," living the moments to their fullest and wishing you had grown up with me, because it was a good life. I hope you enjoy "my side of the story."

Eunice Adkison Padgett (May/June 2013)

HOMEGROWN
ON THE
FARM

MEMORIES FROM THE FARM

*W*hat are memories? The dictionary states they are things remembered, whether good or bad. It is the ability of the mind to retain learned information and knowledge of past events and experiences and to retrieve that information. It is the knowledge or impression that you retain of a person, event, period, or subject. It is the preservation of knowledge and usually the celebration of a deceased person or past event.

In the recent months, while spending time with Daddy I often walked down Memory Lane revisiting "the farm" I knew as a girl. I have questioned Daddy about things, people, and events to see if my memories were correct. I have laughed, cried, and learned. It has been an emotional, sentimental, melancholy, and enlightening experience.

While reflecting on the past, I have been amazed at the many things carried from "the farm" into life. There are many lessons learned as a child and young person that have been given practical application in my adult life.

I feel blessed to have lived in a home full of love and hard work, where life was centered on a great big God. I had parents and siblings that loved deeply. We were a family that worked hard together to see many things accomplished. We served a God that supplied our needs, healed our bodies, answered prayer, and kept us day to day.

I am thankful for the memories of a life filled with love. Of all women, I am abundantly blessed.

The following pages are MY memories; things I have retained through events and experiences in my life while living "on the farm." It is the preservation of the knowledge of those deceased and living as they intertwined in my life. It is the recollection of a mostly happy childhood and lessons learned from those events. These pages reflect feelings and thoughts I have recorded through the years.

These memories are mine. As I share, if you were on "the farm," I am sure memories of your own will come to mind. You will add to my memories and it will become a bigger and better story.

My Parents

I did not have perfect parents, but they were wonderful, praying parents. To my young mind that could be good, and it could be bad, depending on *my* circumstance, desire, and behavior at the time.

Seriously, I am thankful for the prayers of my parents. Healing, intervention from wrong choices, and soul salvation were among the many blessings resulting from their prayers. I am glad God listened and responded to their heart's cry. If a child has praying parents, they cannot ask for a better blessing in life.

My parents loved unconditionally. Their love was strong, deep, and steadfast. No child on earth could have had better parents than me. No, they weren't perfect, but they were THE BEST!

The Siblings

The Adkison family I was born into consisted of one mother, one father, and seven children. An eighth would arrive two years later. JW was the firstborn. He told me someone had said the family was too poor to give him anything but initials for a name. JW was already married and had a child "on the way" by the time I was born. Through my growing years, he was more like an uncle than a brother. His children and I were close to the same age and often had to be corrected for our joint offenses and misbehavior. As I grew older, this changed and we now have a brother/sister relationship that I cherish deeply.

About three years later, another son, Tom was born. Tom was the nurturer. A lot of the time I was his responsibility during my young years, especially after Buddy came along. The year I began school, Tom graduated and was headed for college, the air force, and marriage. He retained his nurturing tendencies for many years by asking about our daily hygiene and proper nourishment. This meant *"did you brush your teeth?"* and *"did you take your vitamins?"*

Approximately three years after Tom's birth another son, Bill came into the world. Bill was the fun-loving, adventurous, and mischievous child—traits he took into his adult world. Bill also loved deeply but tried to make light of his true feelings. He often made sacrifices to see that his youngest sister and brother had the best his dollars could afford. Bill was a people lover and went out of his way to help everyone.

Eighteen months after Bill, a little girl, Ellen, arrived. She was the champion for Buddy and me, her biggest adversary being our next sister, Helen. Ellen was also the more naive of us all, and we often took advantage of her trusting spirit.

Almost two years later, Helen was born. Helen took life head-on. A challenge rarely gave her pause. She loved people and was always finding ways to make their lives better.

Helen was about four years old when Joe came into the family. By blood, Joe is our cousin whose mother had died with tuberculosis. His father was unable to care for him, so my parents adopted him into our family. He was five years old when he became a part of the Adkison family. With Bill, Ellen, Joe, and Helen's ages being so close Mama now had "quadruplets"! Joe was a part of the family before I arrived into this world. He is and always has been my *brother*. I have never thought of him as anything except one of my big brothers.

My childhood memory recalls Joe as the quiet one. Like each of us, he was trying to find his place in the family unit—often questioning authority and at times rebelling. Looking back, I see that his being adopted often caused him to question his position. But to me there never was and never will be a question of his position in the family. He belongs. He always has and always will. He is my brother.

After Helen, I came along. Life in the Adkison family was never the same. Ask any sibling. Helen was seven years old at the time. She had been the baby all those years and I was challenging and changing her position. This age span caused many rifts when we were young. But we lived through those years of trying to find our place within the family and became friends and loving sisters.

I was almost two years old when my little brother, Buddy, was born. He was always my little brother and I did not want anyone annoying him. We had our disagreements, but no one else had better trouble him. This included my mother and father. I received many spankings for interfering with his correction.

Buddy was my playmate and my companion in conspiracy. As we grew older, he proved to be my best friend. He became my advisor and my encourager; the biggest cheerleader in my corner.

When the family moved to the farm, JW and Tom were no longer living in our home. JW was married with a family of his own. Tom was in college and would never again live full time with us. The farm became home to the remaining six siblings. Many fond and pleasant memories fill my mind of our time together. We worked hard, had fun and found adventure through the years as we were growing up on "the farm."

The Farmhouse

I was very young, just entering the first grade, when we first moved to "the farm." The family now living together was Mama and Daddy, two older brothers, two older sisters, a younger brother, and me.

Times were difficult because Daddy had been seriously injured the year I was born. My older brothers worked hard to help "ends meet." I was too young to know this. I never knew how poor we were until I was a teenager. There was food on the table, laughter in the house, and plenty of love to go around. For me, that was enough.

We *really* were poor. We had no indoor plumbing until I was eleven or twelve years old. Just outside the back door was a well. We had a bucket on a rope to draw water. We had a dipper for drinking, but you had best *not* drink from it, get a glass. Our restroom was an outhouse that **was** out in the field—at least it seemed that way. We had to go down a path through the pine trees and behind the barn. At times, it seemed *miles* away, especially at night when none of my siblings wanted to go with me.

Our bathtub was a real bathtub in the yard during the summer months. The winter months called for a wash pan inside the house. We always used hot water for cleaning, whether it was for our bodies, the house or the dishes. Water was drawn from the well, put into pots and heated on the stove. We had a gas stove for many years; it was later replaced with an electric model.

Our house had central heat and air. During the winter, it was central air and, in the summer, central heat. There was no air conditioner or heater. The windows were open during the summer months. For many years, an old woodstove with pipes sticking out the window was our winter heat. We eventually got a "double" fireplace. One side opened into the kitchen and the other into the living room. Daddy later installed wood furnaces. The winter months often found us getting dressed *in* bed because of the cold. I recall many days seeing the fog from my breath. It was that cold! Daddy rose early to get the fire going, but the house was so cold it took hours to get warm enough for comfort. Some days, the only warm spot was directly in front of the fire. Summer was hot but bearable due to window fans.

Mama believed Buddy and I needed our daily vitamins. I seemed to choke on them. There was a table against the wall in the kitchen that held our water bucket, dipper, and drinking glasses. There was also a small open space where the floor and the wall didn't quite meet. Buddy and I would often "take" our vitamins at that table. Somehow the vitamins ended up going through the crack along the floor. We were healthy enough without those added supplements. We had plenty of vegetables, sunshine, and outdoor activity. I don't think Mama ever knew we disposed of those vitamins.

Our house was a good size structure. It contained a large living room, a large open kitchen and dining area, four bedrooms, and one bath. The problem was, for years we could only use three bedrooms and the kitchen because the other rooms were unfinished; one bedroom and the bath held lumber to complete the house.

The roof leaked for a long time, a very long time. When the rain came, we put pots under the leaks to catch the water. Mama prayed for a roof many times. She would think there was enough money from a crop sale or some other business venture to get roof repair supplies. But then, Daddy would have to make a preaching trip instead of purchasing roof repairs. Mama didn't complain, she just kept on praying. When the money was made available, she not only got the roof repaired but the house completed which included a remodeled kitchen with cabinets, indoor plumbing and a bathroom.

Although we lacked normal conveniences, we never lacked for friends filling our home. Daddy and Mama knew how to show hospitality and make folks want to come to our house again and again. It wasn't the conveniences of life or the material things; it was the love, laughter, food, and fellowship that drew people into our home.

Many fond memories of overnight guests, stories told and children playing stay in my mind to this day. Family and friends alike were a part of this home.

I recently took my grandsons to the old home place. I told them stories about Nana being a little girl. I answered many questions that day. They took pictures of me standing where the house once stood. We couldn't revisit the house, but we revisited Nana's childhood.

Mama's Rocking Chair

I don't remember Mama ever without a wooden rocking chair. It usually sat near the dining room table and near the back door. She seldom sat and rocked for pleasure. There was always something needing to be done. Even in the rocking chair she was busy, not wasting a moment.

The sound of peas falling into the pan held in Mama's lap was a common noise throughout my life. There is no way to put a number on the bushel of peas and butter beans that were shelled into that "dish pan" she held in her hands. The peas would be shelled, and then she would sit and look through them to make sure no rotten or bad ones had fallen into the pan. The pile would look fine to me, but her fingers would sift through them and another pan was needed for the bad peas. When all was finished, good peas could be prepared for future use to feed the family.

Countless stitches were made in dress and skirt hems, buttons attached, and lace woven into the fabric of a child's outfit by Mama's hands while sitting in her rocking chair. My own wedding dress was one of those garments lovingly, carefully, and patiently stitched. I can visualize her diligently working the lace overlays and the covered buttons perfectly in place.

The rocking chair is where we would see Mama reading her Bible throughout the day and evening as she had a break from the many chores.

The rocking chair was at its best when a grandbaby was in Mama's arms. She would hold the child close, speak sweet words of endearment into their ears, and cover its face with kisses. The child would soon snuggle into her arms and fall asleep. The babies may not remember the times she held them in the rocking chair, but this mother remembers her children being held by Mama and rocked in her chair.

Mama's Hands

Mama's hands were never still. She was always working at something. The day was full of chores to do, children to tend, and many evenings there were preparations for church.

Making dresses for three growing girls was enough work without all the other chores that had to be done on the farm. Mama made my dresses most of my life. I rarely remember a "store-bought" dress. The first I ever remember having was when I was in the seventh or eighth grade. I don't remember the occasion prompting its purchase.

Mama saved printed fabric flour sacks to make a dress. She would match the patterns each time she bought a bag of flour until there was enough for a dress. When Mama was making a dress, she usually made three, one for each of us girls. She did this for many years. Mama was a very talented seamstress. She believed everything should be neat and done with pride. From the cutting out of the fabric until the last button sewn, it was done neatly and skillfully. I remember watching her rip out many seams until it was like she wanted.

Mama didn't need to buy a pattern to make a dress. My tenth-grade Spanish teacher had some of the cutest clothes. I would come home and tell Mama about them and she would take a pencil and paper and draw until she had it like my teacher's outfit. She would then make a pattern and sew a dress like I had described and desired.

Mama's hands made many quilts. I remember the quilting frame hanging from the rafters in the unfinished living room. She took the time to cut fabric into squares, finding fabric that blended well. She would then sew the squares together until she had enough for the quilt top. Mama would then take the top, the padding and the backing and bring them to the quilting frame for hand stitching. She would sit for hours and painstakingly hand stitch the quilt. She did beautiful work.

Mama loved to bake. Her kitchen was proof of this love. She cooked many cakes and pies for church dinners and bake sales through the years. My son, Greg says one of the fondest memories with his Granny Adkison is standing on a chair at the counter and "helping" her bake cakes. I spent many hours at her house after I was married helping her make small pies to sell as a church fundraiser at the local sewing factory. She made cakes and pies for family gatherings. Thanksgiving was the holiday with the most cakes and pies spread across the table. She made cakes for her church fundraiser until she could no longer stand and do the work. Discontinuing this was one of her greatest disappointments.

Cooking was one of Mama's favorite things. If you loved to eat, she loved to cook for you. The "boys" in the family outdid themselves eating Mama's cooking. When she learned our favorite, she would always try to prepare it when any of us came to see her. Those times of our visits, she made sure I had coconut cake, Greg the lemon cheesecake and Melissa a chocolate. Johnny got her special fried cornbread. She put "love" in her cooking, an ingredient my husband teasingly tells me that I often leave out.

Mama's hands saw many clothes washed. Many years we didn't have a washer and dryer. Washing clothes was done by hand. Her hands hung clothes outside to dry no matter whether it was the coldest or the hottest weather. It was a blessing indeed the day a washer and dryer was brought into our home.

Mama's hands were comforting to a fevered brow, a stubbed toe, or a thorn in the finger. Her hands wiped many tears, dirt, and grime from my face. Mercurochrome, of course had to be applied to almost every "hurt." She took time to tend to those she loved. I remember having "growing pains" as a child. The leg pain was almost unbearable during the night. Although weary from the long day's work, Mama and Daddy would get up and rub my legs until they eased enough for me to sleep. When I had so much trouble with enlarged intestines Mama made sure that I ate the proper food and did her best to make me comfortable.

Mama's hands weren't always so sweet, though. Whenever one of us had misbehaved, she did not hesitate to get a belt or the flyswatter, but more often a switch, and tend to our attitude or behavior that wasn't what it should have been. She was not abusive, but she was thorough when her hands applied the tool of correction.

Mama's hands earned extra money for things that Daddy could not afford to get the family. I recall wanting a fur coat that I had seen in one of the three department stores in our town. With little money available there was no way she could buy it for me. She found extra work to have enough money to put it on layaway. My future mother-in-law helped her "pay it out."

One of the ways that Mama's hands earned a bit of extra money was through meat demonstrations at the Thrift-Way Supermarket. She enjoyed meeting the people as much or more than cooking the meat.

Vegetable preparation, animal care, church work and family care kept Mama's hands busy. The "things" that were in her hands and the chores she accomplished are too numerous to name. But I will never forget the precious, loving, hardworking hands of my mama.

Planting (Seedtime)

Planting season was a busy time. The ground had to be prepared and Daddy was always breaking in "new ground" and adding another crop. We had to get the ground plowed, the limbs removed, rows made, and the seed planted.

After the summer's harvest, Daddy had set aside seed for the following year. He was careful with the seed. He spread it out for drying and then placed it in a jar until the next planting season.

Daddy would go ahead of us on the tractor, preparing the rows for planting. It was a treat when we were allowed to sit with him and *drive* the tractor. Most often though, we would walk behind and plant the seed. We were to be careful with these seed; we couldn't buy more; they were too expensive. Instructions were to not spill them and don't crush them. This was our food for the winter months, well mostly, Daddy also had a winter garden…and a spring garden…and a fall garden. But for the moment we were looking toward summer, so be careful.

The Soil and the Crops

Daddy had a special "ground" where a particular group of seed was to be planted. He understood the soil. The seed needed to be in good ground. The low land was where the okra patch was planted; this land got a lot of water. The corn had its own part of land, as well as the peas, butterbeans and squash. The watermelons, cucumbers and cantaloupe were usually planted "across the branch." The branch was a little brook that ran through the property. These fields were a long way from the house, so Daddy allowed us to drive the tractor or truck to these areas.

The turnips and tomatoes received extra care and were planted nearby for Mama's easy access. If there wasn't enough rain, we were required to water the tomatoes. When they got tall, we would "stake them off" so they would not fall over as they began to yield the heavy fruit. I couldn't understand why I had to help with these since I didn't even like them. But my daddy expected everyone to help with the work of the fields.

For Daddy to get a good yield from the seed he spent a lot of time preparing the ground. It was plowed, stumps and limbs removed, fertilized and plowed some more. Then the seed was carefully planted.

Some seeds were planted with the planter on the tractor, but most often by hand. It was usually Daddy's hands, but sometimes ours.

I'm sure many prayers were prayed for the crops to prosper and yield a bountiful harvest. All Daddy could do was "work" the soil and plant the seed. The rest was up to God, and He always did a good job when it came time to harvest and "put up" the yield.

The Tools

We were taught to take care of the tools. These instruments were a part of our livelihood. We had the tractor, of course. There were all sorts of attachments for the tractor. Included in these were the disk, the plow, the grader, the planter, the rake and others. The garden hand tools consisted of a variety of hoes, shovels, pitchforks, and rakes.

Each of these played an important part in preparing the ground for the seed. Some were used before the seed could be placed in the ground, others were used afterward.

The hoe is the tool I remember the most because it was usually in my hand. Removing weeds from the rows of plants was often my job. I had many blisters to show for my labor!

The rake and pitchfork were usually fall tools. Our house was surrounded on three sides by pine trees. It was Buddy's and my job to rake the straw and place it around the strawberry plants. We enjoyed playing in the straw; it made good jumping piles and forts. But we did not enjoy raking for the strawberries; after all there was a difference between working and playing.

The tools were to be put away after each use. They weren't to be left in the field or the yard. They were too expensive to lose or destroy, therefore needing to be replaced.

The Tractor

What is a farm without a tractor or two? Daddy had several tractors through the years. The one that I remember the most is a John Deere. Daddy would allow us to drive the tractor at times. This was a fun time for us kids and made us feel "grown-up." The tractor was very important to the farm. It required a lot of maintenance because of the constant wear and tear. If something broke on the tractor other necessities would have to be put aside until the tractor was repaired. It was *the* most important piece of equipment on the farm. Daddy's tractor not only helped produce crops for our farm but was also hired out to other farms, giving an extra bit of income for our family.

The Fruit Trees

Fig trees, plum trees, pecan trees, and blueberry trees (bushes) were the fruit bearing trees on our farm.

The fig trees were scattered throughout the yard. The figs would be picked and brought into the house to be washed. Mama would then slow cook them on the stove. They would be put into jars for "canned figs" to be enjoyed the rest of the year. She would freeze the ones she didn't have time to "cook down" and they would be canned later. Her canned figs were delicious.

The plum trees were located on the far side of the pines that were near the house. During their bearing season, we would use a ladder to reach the fruit on the high limbs. Thankfully, even in our falling from a tipped ladder none of us had any serious injuries. These plums were delicious straight from the tree. A few bushels would be sold but most would be taken to the house for our personal use. Mama would slow cook the plums, using the juice to make jelly. Jelly was a staple on our table; it might be plum, blueberry, blackberry, strawberry, or figs.

The blueberry trees (bushes) were a money-making crop. These delicious berries were picked early in the morning or late in the evening. Mama and Daddy would tell us to not eat them all, some needed to go into the basket to be sold to the local grocery stores or "home" customers.

The pecan trees were in the middle of several crops and were a blessing during gardening season because they provided shade for us hot, hard working farm hands. The pecans had to be handpicked from the ground, taken home, cracked, and "looked." They were then put into the freezer for future use. Many cakes and pies were made with the fruit from these pecan trees.

The blackberries came from the briars that grew throughout the farm. They were a natural fruit that we enjoyed. Aside from the scratches we received and the few snakes we saw, this fruit brought pleasure when in season because they were delicious straight from the bush, in pies and ice cream.

The fruit bearing trees called for hard work. But it was well worth the energy, time and effort when the moment came for us to sit down at the table for one of Mama's meals. We would eat a biscuit full of jelly, a side of canned figs or a cake or pie filled with pecans. Mama made all the work on the farm worthwhile when she would call, "Come eat!"

Sharecropping and Feeding the Multitudes

My experience with sharecropping was not from renting the land but *sharing* our crops with *everyone* in town and all the outreaching communities. Daddy believed in sharing. No one ever came to our house and left empty handed. There was always a jar of homemade jelly, homemade pickles, a slab of meat or a "hamper" of fresh produce given to them to take home.

My parent's motto was "Feed the Hungry" before that organization ever existed. We had our own "Feed the Hungry" nonprofit organization of eight members.

Daddy believed in the pressed down, shaken together, and running over kind of bushel, peck, or basket. I remember picking peas, coming to the end of the row with a full hamper, only to have Daddy meet me there, shake it, and press it down. He would then say, "Now go finish filling it." Off I would go again, filling the basket, meeting him again only to have him say, "Now go pick enough to top it off!"

We got up early, early, early during blueberry season. He wanted us in the blueberry patch while the dew was still on the ground and the sun not yet hot. We would pick those little things and fill our basket. Daddy would come along and want us to add a few more. He would often remind us of "the good measure" Bible verse.

I can truly say my parents had giving hearts. They were true sharecroppers. I think (and believe that I am correct) they gave away much more than they sold or kept. But like Daddy said, "God loves a cheerful giver." He was one cheerful giver of the abundance that we were blessed with from God.

The Barn

The barn was a huge cinder block building. It often stored old furniture, a few tools and lumber from old buildings Daddy had torn down. This lumber was to be used to build chicken coops, sheds for animals, the smokehouse, and whatever else Daddy needed on the farm.

One day, Daddy, Bill, and I were moving some of the lumber. Daddy turned as I was handing him a piece of the lumber and it hit his chin, knocking out two of his lower front teeth. I know it had to hurt, but he didn't complain. While it was healing, he would entertain the younger children, showing them how the watermelon juice would spray out the hole in his chin. They found it quiet intriguing.

During the later summer months, it was Buddy's and my job to get the dried corn from the fields and into the barn. Winter was on its way and the animals would need food. It seemed to take forever to fill the barn to Daddy's approval.

Not too long ago, I went to the barn to get a piece of my mother's furniture. I was surprised at how small the building was now. The barn of my childhood was surely much larger than the one I was standing in! The barn was about a third of the size my mind recalled.

Things look much different in the mind of a ten-year-old than seen by an adult.

No Need for Hired Hands

My parents didn't need hired hands. This is what I often told them—and got into much trouble for saying so. I would say, "You raised eight kids just so you could have help on this farm." I might still argue it to be a truth.

Samson didn't have anything on the younger Adkison children. When cane-grinding time arrived, Daddy didn't use the mule because we didn't own one. He hitched us kids to the beam and around and around and around we would go. It was fun for a while but would soon become tiring. It was a good thing he had more than one child to "hitch up." If it wasn't needed somewhere else that day, Daddy would use the tractor. We felt privileged and safe to drive the tractor when he hooked it to the cane mill; after all we were only going in a circle. It was a joyous day when he bought a riding lawnmower and allowed us to use it for cane grinding.

We really weren't mistreated or abused. We were treated with respect and kindness. Daddy and Mama just expected us to help carry the load of the farm. In our youth, we had no idea how large the load was for them.

The Swing

If you walked out the back door, turned left, took the path through the pine trees, go past the plum orchard on the left and whatever crop (usually corn) might be growing on the right, and walk for a bit you would arrive at the pecan "orchard." Hanging from a big rope attached to a large tree limb would be a swing. At times this might be a swing with a wooden seat, but most often it would be a tire swing.

Many hours were spent on these swings. It was a time of play with my siblings and nieces. We would get on the swing and someone would push us to the sky! They would spin us around until we became dizzy and crying, "Stop!" Laughter and squeals could be heard through the fields. Occasionally, one of us would fall and get a little banged up, but we would soon climb back on the swing for another ride.

These swings also provided a place to go for thinking, reading and detachment from the busy world around us, if only for a few moments. The tree swing was a place of relaxation for the weary. This was also a place of refuge, quietness and healing for the many emotions in life. It was a place for us to cry when we were sad, hurt or disappointed without fear of being seen or heard. It was a refuge for us to simmer in our anger, allowing Time to be the avenger and not us.

Somehow sitting in the swing, slowly kicking the dirt, making marks with the toe or shoe that only I knew what was written, provided solace and relief for this girl. It was a safe place for a young lady desperately needing an outlet for emotions that could not be bottled up and contained for long.

I still enjoy a good swing, kicking the dirt, writing in the sand, and flying high in the sky!

The Back Porch

Our house had two porches, a front and a back. The front was seldom used; friends and family always came to the back door. The back porch was a place of busy-ness. This is where much farm activity took place.

We would get up early and head to the fields with Daddy. The harvest needing to be picked was where we would go. It may be peas, butterbeans, squash, corn, tomatoes, or whatever. We would pick and pick, then Daddy would take the produce to the back porch and leave it for Mama to begin cleaning or shelling. When he would get the porch floor about half full, he would bring us home to begin helping Mama. He would then return to the field for more produce.

With all my complaining these were good days. We would sit around the pile of vegetables with a pan in our lap or a knife in our hand, working hard. These times gave us opportunity for a lot of conversation. We discussed everything in life. We would laugh, cry and even complain. We solved a lot of issues while sitting around those piles of vegetables.

The complaining usually came in the late afternoon. We had gotten up early, worked in the sun and then sat long hours preparing vegetables for future meals and we were tired. The pile would begin to look like we were going to finish soon, but Daddy would come in with another hamper full, dump it on the floor and expect it to be completed soon. There was much sighing and complaining, "Daddy, why more?"

He would just say, "We have to get this crop in before it goes to waste." He would then head back to the field. After several times of this he would see we were about finished and he would say, "One more bushel and we will stop for the day." Those were the most beautiful words ever spoken, at least to those of us working on the back porch.

Canning, Freezing, and Eating

When we finished on the back porch it didn't mean that we were finished for the day. The vegetables were brought into the house to be "looked." This means we took any bad ones out that were missed while working on the back porch. Next, they had to be washed, several times. We would then "blanch" them, cool them, pour them into freezer bags and place them inside a large chest freezer.

If the vegetables weren't going into the freezer, they were prepared for canning. This process required washing and sterilizing the jars, filling them with vegetables, placing them in the canner on the stove and praying really hard that it didn't explode. The jars then had to cool and be taken to the barn or shed for storage, waiting for winter use.

The best part of gardening was eating the harvest. There was nothing as good as Mama's fresh summer vegetables. She loved to cook, and we could taste the "love" with which she seasoned every meal. With a hardworking, hungry and growing bunch around the table we seldom had leftovers. Those gathered at the table usually consisted of our family (by then seven of us) and whatever company might have shown up to help for the day.

After supper, there were dishes to wash, the back porch must be swept and emptied of pea shells or corn husks or whatever was left from the day's work. Then there was prayer to be said and baths to be taken before we could call it a day. We would then get up the next morning and begin the process again.

It seems Mama and Daddy never got tired. I know they did, we just never saw it nor heard them complain. They were still working when I went to bed and were "up and at it" when I would get up the next morning. When did they rest? I didn't know how to appreciate their work efforts and ethics back then.

It is a time I will never forget. The hard work and the companionship are memories that remain today in my mind and heart.

Isn't One Farm Enough?

The farm acreage was vast to my young eyes and body. Daddy planted crops of every kind in every season. The workday was long; it began early and ended late but was productive. Food was plentiful on the farm.

We grew tomatoes on the farm. We planted, watered and picked these tomatoes. They were mainly for meals instead of "putting up." Most of the family enjoyed tomato sandwiches or even green, fried tomatoes. Yet our farm seemed to not produce the tomatoes Daddy wanted or thought we needed. So off we would go north of town to the Padgett farm (some distant kin to my husband) to get *more*! Buckets, bushels, and tubs of tomatoes were picked and brought home.

We would go to the local cannery, wash and sterilize Mason canning jars. The tomatoes would then be washed, boiled, peeled, and placed into the clean jars. The jars would be carefully placed into a large canner for "canning." Stewed tomatoes and tomato juice were the end product. To my young mind's way of thinking, there would be enough for the entire community.

This was a long hot day consisting of an early trip to the Padgett farm then to the cannery. This was also a dangerous process. The canners or the jars could explode. Thankfully, this only happened a very few times. I don't remember any burns or cuts.

The work was hard, but the convenience of homegrown tomatoes, tomato sauce, and tomato juice were worth the hours of the hard labor involved. These jars of canned goodness were a blessing for the rest of the year.

A day at the cannery also provided a day of conversation. It offered an opportunity for family and friends to be together, work and talk about life.

Farm Animals

A farm isn't a farm unless it has a few animals. We had an abundance of animals on our farm. We had animals for food and animals for pets.

Hogs were a staple at our farm. Daddy would keep the hogs out near the barn, a good distance from the house. It was often my job to feed these smelly animals. One day while feeding them I observed the birth of several pigs. That was amazing to a young girl. I never minded slaughter day until those little pigs, that had grown up to be hogs, had to be taken down.

Slaughter day was a busy day with a lot of people on hand to help. It was an opportunity for family and friends to visit while doing a day of hard work.

First, a fire was built and a huge black cast iron pot full of water was placed on top of the fire. Then the hog was killed. The scalding hot water was poured over it to help the hair come off easier. The hog was then scraped clean of its hair. Next it was gutted, washed, and brought inside to be cut up and the meat prepared for freezing. The "chittlins" were cleaned and cooked, creating a horrible smell in the house. Mama usually found someone to take these to keep them out of her kitchen.

Part of the meat was made into sausage. We had a grinder the meat was put through and then seasoned. The next step was someone holding the "casing" while another machine stuffed the meat. This was usually a job for the younger children. A fire would be built in the smokehouse. Daddy and my brother Bill would be up all night checking on the meat that was being smoked. We had some good eating for several days after slaughter day.

We also had chickens. We had baby chickens (biddies), roosters, hens and eggs. The chicken coop was another smelly place. I did not enjoy cleaning it or gathering the eggs. Chickens bite—or peck—or whatever, their attacks hurt. When Mama decided to have chicken for a meal, she would go out to the chicken yard, which was a fenced area around the chicken coup, and catch a chicken. She was good at catching them and wringing their necks. We watched as the chicken would flop around on the ground for a while. When it was dead, she would take the feathers off with hot water, clean it good and then it was cooked. No one could fry chicken like Mama! The older chickens went into dumplings and rice dishes.

We sometimes had cows, although they weren't as frequent on the farm as the hogs and chickens. Daddy worked as a produce manager in a grocery store for several years. He would bring the "bad" produce home to the animals. I remember one cow that he fed onions. The cow loved those things. She would eat them as fast as he could feed them to her. When we slaughtered the cow the onion taste was so strong, we were unable to eat the meat. Lesson learned: never feed your cow or any other slaughter animal onions.

At one point, we had goats. Mama bottle fed some of the baby goats. She enjoyed her time with those babies. They are some of the cutest yet most obnoxious and ornery creatures on earth. I recall one day the goats got out and we were trying to get them back into the pen. Betty, my sister-in-law, had left her trailer door open when she came out to help and one of the goats got inside her trailer house! She was fit to be tied (Betty, not the goat); she was not at all happy.

We rarely had horses. I remember one horse and one pony. These animals took too much time, care and food, producing nothing but a pet. We could not afford this luxury.

We did have dogs and cats, although they were outside pets only! Daddy and Mama rarely allowed these inside the house. Sometimes on cold winter nights, we could bring a kitten inside to play with for a little while. My favorite cat was a grey one, her name was Bright Eyes. She was hit several times by cars. One night as we were on our way to church a car hit her. Daddy said, "We will take care of her when we get home." We thought she was dead, but when we got home, she was okay. This happened several times to our amazement. A snake bit her and caused her eye to pop out. Daddy did surgery on the eye and allowed me to keep her. I believe he was a bit partial to that old cat himself.

One of our favorite animals was a dog, named Trixie. She was a dark German shepherd. My brother Buddy and I played with her for hours at a time. She was so smart. We would play baseball and Trixie would catch the ball, chase us around the bases, sometimes blocking our way because she "knew" we were "out." It was a sad day when she died. Daddy always allowed us to have a pet on the farm for fun times such as these.

Hoes, Water, Wood, and Ditches

Hoes, water, wood, and ditches were our main toys while living on the farm. We had no money for store bought toys, so we made our own most of the time.

We had a big backyard with a good dirt drive. This drive was the home of grand castles, mountains, rivers, roads and raceways. All the imagination needed was a good garden hoe and a few pieces of wood. Buddy and I would use the hoe to make roads, dig holes and ditches. These holes and ditches were filled with water. The holes became lakes and the ditches were rivers. A piece of wood was laid across the ditch for a bridge. Our "cars and trucks" were smaller pieces of wood. We had some great times on these little roads in the backyard.

The Swimming Hole

Summers were hot on the farm and the dirt was dirty. These two things alone were enough to make a trip to the swimming hole *the event* of the day.

Every spring, Daddy and the "boys" would take the tractor and other equipment to the creek behind my brother, JW's house and clean out the swimming hole. Winter rains had caused limbs and debris to accumulate and need to be removed.

The swimming hole was deep. We had a rope to swing out into the creek. A diving board was on the opposite side of the creek from the house. To get to the diving board, we had a choice, either swim across or take the time to cross a shallow place with a lot of rock then climb the bank. It was necessary to climb the bank either way.

A large soapstone ran across one side of the swimming hole. We would swim there, rest awhile and dive or jump from the stone.

Most of us learned to swim by being tossed into the hole. I wasn't so lucky. I didn't allow them to toss me in, so I didn't learn to swim until years later and then not as well as the other children. I always had an "inner tube" nearby to assist me in the deep water. Although I could "dog paddle" pretty good.

Most days, Daddy would give us an hour to take a break from the farm work to swim. We knew exactly how long it took to run the quarter mile. We made good use of our time for that hour.

Our family did not allow "mixed bathing." The young boys could swim with us girls until about twelve years of age. Unfortunately, Buddy was usually the only boy around. He enjoyed Sunday afternoons because it was men's day at the creek, and he didn't have to swim alone.

One of my favorite times of all was when Mama would take a few minutes from her busy work to join us at the swimming hole. For some reason, I was always amazed that she could swim. I guess it was because it was such a rare occasion when she could join us in the fun.

Those days of swimming in Panther Creek are some of the fondest of my childhood. I still enjoy opportunities to jump into a pool, which I much prefer now days.

Bringing Friends Home

I sometimes had to think twice before bringing friends home. There were several given factors to consider:

Number 1. The house was not normal. It was unfinished, no hot water and no plumbing, plus other embarrassing things.
Number 2. The home was not normal. We had rules, work, prayer and God-talk.
Number 3. Daddy would *ask* questions.

When my friends, or those of my siblings, arrived we had our first awkward moments of introduction and them becoming adjusted to our home. We would then play, talk, do our homework and whatever friends did in those days.

At mealtime, we would have the blessing, eat, talk and laugh. Somewhere during that time Daddy would begin his questions. "Now, who is your daddy?" "Who is your mother, what was her maiden name?" I would sit there thinking *"Daddy, why do you* always *do this?* One thing was always a surety, Daddy would eventually find someone in their family that he knew and may even figure out how we could be kinfolk.

Then evening would come, and we would begin preparing for bed. Daddy would call us either into the dining room or the living room for family prayer. I would think *"Oh no, what are my friends going to think now?"*

The next day, we would go back to school or Daddy would take my friends home. I was so sure they would never want to come home with me again. Yet every friend that came to my house would tell me how much fun it was being there, how much they enjoyed it and couldn't wait to come back. I could breathe! They liked this family that I thought so unusual.

The Thief!

My daddy loves people. He loves to socialize and have conversation. No matter where he goes or who he sees he will soon strike up a conversation with someone. By living in the same small town for so many years almost everyone knows him and will take time to "visit" when they see him around town.

Through the years, he would stop to get fuel for the automobile, or pick up eggs, milk or a loaf of bread. Daddy would "get to talking" and walk out without payment. When he got home, he would realize this and say, "Oh my, I was talking and walked right out without paying." He would call or go back to the place of business and they would say, "Oh, Mr. John, we knew you would remember it after a while and return to pay." His honesty and integrity had made a reputation for him; people weren't concerned that he would take advantage of them.

Several years ago, Tom was visiting Daddy and had left his wallet on the chest of drawers. Later in the day he couldn't find it and began to question where it might have been misplaced. That evening preparing for bed, Daddy emptied his pockets and there was Tom's wallet. He had picked it up thinking it was his, telling Tom all day, "I have my wallet, but I don't know what happened to yours."

A few months later, I was in DeFuniak cleaning our rental house. I had called Mama and Daddy to let them know I would be in town but would not have time to go visit. I suggested meeting them for lunch after their doctor's appointments.

They finished with the doctor and came out to the house to pick me up for lunch. I noticed they were in a different car than theirs and questioned them about it. Daddy said, "It is Tammi's *(my niece)* car. The air conditioner isn't working in her car and she needed to go to Crestview for a doctor's appointment, so I told her to take mine." Mama spoke up and said, "She sure needs to pick up all those papers scattered across the back seat, no one can sit back there."

As we prepared to leave for lunch Daddy handed me the keys to drive. The keys wouldn't fit into the ignition. I said, "These keys don't work." He said, "Well, they are the keys Tammi gave me this morning." I looked around and saw some keys in the console, tried them in the ignition and they worked. He couldn't figure out where he had gotten two sets of keys.

We went for lunch and had a good visit. They came back to the house and stayed a bit then headed home. I left later that evening after completing my cleaning.

Not long after I got home, Tammi called and said, *"Aunt Eunice, you know the car that Papa was driving today?"*

I said, "Yes, Papa said it was yours."

Laughing, she said, *"Well, it wasn't mine. I met Papa coming in the drive as I was going out and asked him what he had done with my car. He told me, "This is your car."*

I told him, *"No, Papa, that isn't my car."*

He asked me, *"Well, whose car do I have then?"*

I told him, *"I have no idea."*

I called Thriftway and told Bill that Papa had someone's car and had no idea to whom it belonged. Bill said he had heard on the police scanner about a vehicle being stolen. Papa called the police station and told them that he most likely had the "stolen" car, but he was busy preparing for the church steak supper and couldn't bring it to them at this time but would come in a while. They said, "Mr. Adkison, you just stay where you are, and we will come get the car." Tammi and I were laughing so much by this point that we could barely speak. She then explained, "Papa and Granny had come out of the doctor's office and not being used to my car had gotten into a white car parked next to mine. The keys had been left in the ignition, so Papa had started it and gone to my house."

The car belonged to someone our family knew and of course the local police knew Daddy wouldn't intentionally steal an automobile. This theft became the "talk of the town" for a few days. We have laughed about this messy, stolen car so many times during these past years.

I now tease Daddy about being a thief. I tell him, "After all the years of teaching us to be honest and upright citizens you are becoming a known thief around town." I say to him, "First, you steal gasoline, then milk, eggs, and bread. Then you begin stealing wallets and not "owning up" to the theft. Now you are stealing cars. We don't want to have to visit you in jail these last years that you have left here on earth."

We give him a hard time for his statement to the police about not having *time* to take the stolen car to the police station because he was *too busy* at the moment. Only my daddy could get away with something like this! Because of his reputation and Godly character, Daddy's integrity had a voice of its own. I have teasingly labeled him an "honest thief."

The Fishing Hole

Occasionally, Daddy would take us across the road from the farmhouse to the "fishing hole." The fishing poles had to be outfitted with the right hook, line, sinker and bobber. Then we would dig in the yard for the fish bait, which were wiggler worms. When we had enough, we would begin tromping through the woods. It was not an easy trek for us girls with our skirts. The briars seemed to cling to our bare legs. We didn't fuss too much because it was a rare treat to go fishing with Daddy. Before we got to our fishing spot, we had to cross a log that spanned a stream. Walking this log was always a bit scary to me. I was careful to not make it a big deal because I didn't want to be sent home. It seemed to take forever to get to the fishing spot, but after I got older and went with Daddy it wasn't all that far in reality.

As we approached the "fishing hole" Daddy would begin telling us to be quiet, that our noise would hinder the fish from biting. What child wants to be quiet when there are so many questions to ask? Daddy wasn't too harsh and would allow us to talk quietly. I don't remember if we caught a lot of fish. The memories I have are the trips through the woods and the time spent with Daddy. He made time for us kids, whether boy or girl.

What? You Don't Have a TV?

There has never been a television in my parent's home. Well, there was for a short time. My sister brought hers when she moved back home from a difficult marriage. It was in her bedroom and was not supposed to be plugged in for use. We did hook it up a couple of times, but the rabbit ear antennas would only allow us to pick up a station for a little while. This was done when we knew Mama and Daddy would be out of the house for a *long* time. It was quickly gotten rid of because Daddy had purposed in his heart to not allow its influence in our lives and home.

Daddy felt most television programs portrayed the things he taught against to be the norm of a household and a life. The list of negative influences was long. The commercials were advertising products with which he did not agree and did not allow us to partake. He would say, "I won't allow that kind of behavior, talk and actions in my home from the people that live here or visit so why would I want to have someone in a box doing it every day?"

He taught against attending movie theaters and saw no difference in the two except you went out and paid to watch the theater and the TV was a permanent fixture in the home. He also felt it was a waste of precious time with little or no benefit.

My friends and extended family would ask if I had seen a program. I would say, "No, we don't have a TV." They would then look at me as if I had become some kind of freak. It made me feel awkward, but I told them my daddy and mama didn't approve of them. This led to more questions, some I could answer and some I couldn't.

I can truthfully say that we weren't deprived of entertainment or socially handicapped by the absence of the television in our home. We had family games and interaction. Daddy was very well-informed about life, politics and the daily happenings in the world and our community. We didn't live in such a sheltered environment that we missed out on anything. He did this for our mental, emotional, and spiritual protection.

Today, I am thankful I didn't have the influence of the ungodly actions and speech of those programs. I'm thankful my mind was not bombarded with the promotion of alcohol and cigarette use and the promiscuity of the world. I appreciate that my parents could look ahead and realize the damage television can have on the family. They made the wise decision for our well-being.

These same reasons are the basis on which my husband and I decided and chose to not have a television in our home negatively influencing us, our children, and our grandchildren. We are informed and stay on top of the events of the world around us but guard against its influence in our lives.

Toys

There wasn't much money available when I was a child for much of anything except the necessities of life. Toys were not necessities, yet with a little imagination we had plenty of things with which to play.

Buddy and I had Matchbox cars before Matchbox cars were invented. We would take empty matchboxes, cut wheels from cardboard and use straight pins to attach the wheels to our vehicle. We would open the box a bit and it became a "truck."

Paper dolls were one of our favorite toys, at least they were my favorite; Buddy didn't mind joining in most of the time. The sales papers in the mail were a wonderful way to get free paper dolls, cutting out the men, women, boys, and girls. Cardboard became designer sofas, chairs, houses, churches, church pews or whatever was needed. I remember many "church services" with those paper dolls, they were the most "churched" people in the world, and they were wonderful "worshippers."

Most of our toys were sticks, rocks or whatever we could find to make a toy. Our imaginations could bring most anything to life.

Sticks became pistols and guns, a sword, fishing poles, or a spear. Pine straw was forts and castles. Rocks were grenades, marbles, and other needed items.

Among the very few store-bought toys I recall is a baby doll. Somehow, her tummy got smashed, but we taped her together and with clothes on she looked fine. Since the poor thing was already "busted," it made it easier for Dr. Buddy and Nurse Eunice to perform the many necessary surgeries.

One Christmas, Bill gave me a beautiful bride doll that not only walked but threw her bouquet. He gave Buddy a remote-controlled, red convertible Corvette. We played for hours with these toys and took very good care of them. They lasted for years.

Christmas

Christmas meant family at our house, not gifts. I remember very few gifts that I received. I know there were gifts under the tree because I recall seeing them. I also saw my sister, Ellen "peeking" in the packages. I cannot recollect what most packages contained except a bride doll that Bill bought me and a Barbie doll coloring book I kept for years. Many happy hours were spent playing "make-believe" with that wonderful doll and book.

The things I remember most is bundling up in our heavy coats and going to the woods with Daddy to choose the grandest tree, Mama having hot chocolate and a dessert for us when we got back, making homemade decorations together, and lots of laughter. The day was one of the few occasions Daddy took time from work to be with us kids, making the season so special. I didn't realize even this outing was work for him.

Christmas was the one time of the year our house looked so pretty, even though everything was homemade. After Ellen and Helen got jobs, they saved their money and bought "fancy" decorations. Now, all these years later I realize it was the love and family time that made it so beautiful.

After the tree was decorated, we would all get in the car and drive through the small town looking at the lights in everyone's yard.

There is a perfect circled lake in the middle of my hometown and those Colonial style houses would be gorgeously decorated for the community to enjoy.

One stop was always at the Courthouse. A huge Nativity scene was in the courtyard every year. It was a reminder to all passing by the reason the season was to be celebrated.

At some time during the weeks leading to Christmas Day, there would be a special church service and all the children would receive a gift of an orange, apple and some nuts. We would read the Christmas story and sing carols.

Christmas began on Christmas Eve. There was family arriving from out of town, gifts exchanged and friends dropping by. Christmas morning would begin with a house filled with family and friends. The guys would go hunting and the girls would help Mama prepare the midday meal. Dinner time (lunch) would find us all with plates piled high with food and desserts. The rest of the day would be filled with lots of laughter and storytelling.

The Christmas season was a special time for family and friends. "Things" I don't remember, but the gift of family, the gift of sharing, and the gift of a Savior have stayed in my memory and become the most important Christmas gifts of all and remain so today.

The Children and a Few of Their Escapades

The Adkison children were not angels. Sorry, I didn't mean to disappoint you with that bit of information. Their daddy was a preacher, but it took his children many years to become "saints."

Our days were full of adventures of some kind. When children range in the ages we were; one or two were going through either a rebellious or an adventurous stage. Most often, thankfully, it was seeking adventure. You see, the farm where we lived was ten miles from a very small town. Adventure had to be *made* if there was any.

As a very small girl I remember my brother, Bill, "hanging" our grandmother from the rafters. The house was not completed. Several rooms had the open rafter look before it became so popular. Granny

Rushing became ill, so Mama brought her to our house for a few days. I believe she was feeling more lonely than ill. Her bed was set up in the living room. One day she was feeling well enough to be a bit cranky. Bill, the most mischievous of the eight, got a rope, tied it to Granny's ankles, threw it over the open rafter and began to pull the rope just enough to raise her legs a bit. She began to holler at my mother and daddy, "Bessie! John! I'm gonna kill him, I'm gonna kill him!" Mama came in and "rescued" Granny, told Bill to behave, then went back to the kitchen and had a good laugh.

Daddy had gone "gopher digging" and had gotten several gophers. These are a type of land terrapin and people in our community love to eat them. For some reason they had died. My two sisters, Ellen and Helen, took the dead gophers and strategically placed them alongside the busy highway. They then hid to see what would happen as people passed by. Cars and trucks began to pass the house. Seeing the gophers at the edge of the road, they would slam on brakes, jump out of their automobiles, grab one and head back to their car. They would then realize the thing was dead and put it back beside the road. Many of the people became frustrated. One man especially did not appreciate their prank. A utility truck loaded with pipe came to a screeching stop when he spotted them. As he slammed on the brakes the pipe slid off the truck onto the road. Dead gophers and a highway strewn with pipe did not make a happy afternoon for a weary worker. My sisters felt bad about that one and did away with the gophers, at Daddy's insistence I am sure.

My sisters often had their disagreements. Many times, it was because Ellen defended something Buddy and I had done. I remember one morning very vividly. Mama and Daddy had left early to go on their produce sales route. The bus would be by in about an hour to pick up the four of us for school. Ellen and Helen got into an argument about something to do with Buddy and me. The argument quickly became a fight. Ellen emptied the bookcases by throwing books at Helen. I had a wooden drum major baton and one of them broke it on the other's elbow. The bus arrived, and we had to go to school. We were all in big trouble when we got home from school and faced our parents with a messy living room.

One evening, Mama and Daddy were late getting home from their produce route. Ellen, Helen, Bill, and Joe got into a fight. Their wrestling caused the back door to come out of the frame. That was bad, but worse, the door was falling toward the wood heater. Thankfully, they caught it and managed to get it into place without causing a fire. There was a major discussion around the table that evening about fussing, fighting and carefulness in the house.

One of the things we enjoyed as children was jumping off the roof of the chicken coop. Of course, this was prohibited for safety reasons. To us kids, this prohibition meant it was okay if our parents didn't see us. While Mama and Daddy were on their produce sales route, we would place a "watchman" at the end of the lane. This watchman would give us warning of Mama and Daddy's arrival. We didn't understand they were trying to keep us from the danger of getting hurt; we only believed they were keeping us from something fun.

Curfew was 10:00 PM for us girls. I don't believe the boys had one, if so, it was *not* 10:00 PM. Ellen and Helen thought this was not fair, especially when Bill would come home at a much later hour. One night, they had the idea of letting Mama and Daddy know just how late he was arriving home. They didn't realize Mama and Daddy never went into a good sleep until they knew all of us were safely in our beds. The girls took a cowbell and hooked it up where it would make a crashing, loud noise when Bill opened his bedroom door. Bill was so mad at the girls, but it made them feel a bit compensated for his late arrival.

There are many more escapades that we got into, especially the older children. I can't recount many of their tales and mischievous exploits; I wasn't around or was too young. But if you are ever at the table when it is "table talk time" you just might hear about some of them.

Hunting and Fishing Days (and Nights)

Wildlife played a big part in our life on the farm. Daddy and the "boys" would often hunt squirrel, deer and wild hog. This was not only done for pleasure but to help put food on the table for a hungry and growing family.

In February, when the dogwood trees began to bloom, Daddy and the "boys" would go sucker gigging. A sucker is a type of fish that would come into the creek this time of the year. The fishing was done at night and the water was still very cold. Poor boys didn't own waders; they just stayed in the water until their feet and legs became numb enough to enjoy the outing. A gig is a pronged, fork contraption on a long handle. A gas pump-up lantern would be held in one hand and the gig in the other. When a school of sucker fish would come by, they would be stabbed with the gig then brought home for cleaning and eating. On one of these trips my brother, Bill mistook his cold foot for a fish and pierced it with the gig. It made for a good story but not a good feeling. Upon arriving home, the "boys" were thankful Mama had a good fire going and hot chocolate on hand after this chilly outing.

Thanksgiving was a day of family, fun, laughter and a big squirrel hunt. The entire clan, the children, the in-laws and those soon to be in-laws, gathered together early at my parents' house before dawn. Mama would cook a huge breakfast for everyone, and the boys would head to the woods after the meal.

A squirrel hunt involved going deep into the woods to find the squirrels. At times the hunters would take a dog. Someone would find a vine coming down the tree and begin shaking it, causing the squirrels to scurry around the branches. The hunters would begin shooting the squirrels and this process would go on for most of the morning. There was much hollering and laughter coming through those woods during this time.

My daddy loved to eat squirrel meat. My soon-to-be husband was careful to shoot the squirrel in the head to save the body from mutilation. My daddy informed him to never again shoot a squirrel in the head because that was his favorite part of the eating.

The group would come back to the house for dinner. The midday meal at our house was called dinner and the evening meal was supper. The boys would clean the squirrels while the women were finishing up dinner. A big meal was eaten; tales of the morning hunt would be told, and laughter was plentiful. Later in the evening the "boys" would either return for another squirrel hunt or go deer hunting.

Christmas afternoon was another time for hunting. As the family began to marry there weren't quite as many participants due to many spending the day elsewhere with their families. Those that came to hunt enjoyed Mama's cooking, the hunting, fellowship, and laughter.

The hog hunting was an event filled with tales of chasing hogs, misfired guns, hogs chasing the "boys" and wild truck rides. Most often the hogs were brought home and put in a pen to be "domesticated" until butchering day. Sometimes they were shot in the field and the meat brought home for processing. Dogs were normally used to assist in these hunts.

There were other times of hunting and fishing during the year, but Thanksgiving and Christmas were times the entire family came together to enjoy the activities.

The Cars

Of all the vehicles that my parents owned I can only remember three. The first was the red Triumph Estate Wagon. We were in desperate need of transportation. A local grocery store was giving a car away through a drawing. Daddy put his name in the drawing and then told us he was going to win the car. We still attended the old church building "in town" and had to pass the grocery store each time we went to church. As we passed Daddy would say, "There's my car." Sure enough, when the drawing took place, my daddy was the winner. This was a lesson in faith to me as a child. God knows our needs and He will supply.

The second car I remember well is the blue station wagon. I don't remember the model or make. I do remember it was used for everything. Mama and Daddy used it for their produce route, the back holding quite a lot of produce. It was used for transportation to the grocery store, the laundromat, church functions and "Convention." The rear seat faced the back window. This was usually where Buddy and I sat.

Traveling the three hundred miles to Ocala, Florida, where we met for the Convention, was an adventure. Mama would pack our clothes and a large picnic lunch. We would pile into the car and take off. Buddy and I would be facing the rear and we pulled quite a few pranks on those traveling behind. Our favorite thing was to get the eighteen-wheelers to blow their big horn for us. We would make a fist and pump our arm. In a bit the driver would blow his horn. We would do this until Mama or Daddy told us to stop.

About halfway to Ocala, Daddy would pull into a roadside park under a huge moss-covered oak tree. Mama would get out the picnic basket and make banana or tomato sandwiches for lunch. This also gave us children time to run off some energy before getting back into the car.

I remember one year the fumes from the car were so bad we could hardly breathe. I don't know what the problem was, but we couldn't roll the rear window down. It was a very hot and miserable trip that year, due to the car having no air conditioning.

The other car was a grey Buick. Daddy helped Ellen and Helen purchase this car. It was "their" car for work and visiting friends. After the girls married the car became Daddy's. This is the car in which I learned to drive.

Shortly after I got my driver's license, we were going to Caryville, Florida, to a revival service and Daddy allowed me to drive. As I was approaching a curve, I didn't slow down enough to make the turn. It had been raining and a dirt road led straight off the curve. Daddy (and Mama) said, "Slow down." I hit the brakes but also hit the clay that had washed onto the road. This led to me overcorrecting and landed us in the ditch; the car actually straddled the ditch. We were unhurt, but we had to call someone to help get us out and did not make it to the revival service that night. After this incident, Mama was a bit nervous for a while but continued to allow me to drive. The car and I had an understanding; me being very careful behind its wheel.

Boys, War, Worries, and Prayer…

I had three siblings in the armed forces, two in the Army and one in the Air Force. Tom served a tour in Greenland, Joe a tour in

Germany, and Bill in Vietnam. I was seven years old when Tom joined the Air Force in 1961. He served four years and was discharged on a Friday in August 1965. Bill was called to duty the following Monday. Joe and Bill were both serving in foreign lands at the same time.

Bill was drafted into the Army and Joe joined. Joe desired to serve as helicopter gunner. His records showed him an only child; therefore, he was not allowed to serve in Vietnam (my parents adopted him but retained his given name). My parents were thankful; one son at war was enough.

Of the three, Bill's tour is the most vivid in my memory because the United States was at war with Vietnam and the danger for our men was great. We also lived near Eglin Air Force Base and heard the daily practice of the jet planes flying overhead. There was much concern for all three of the boys due to the state of our nation. Thankfully, Tom and Joe were serving in "friendly" areas. We often had "prayer breaks" during the day for these loved ones.

I will always remember the day Bill left home for Vietnam. It was a day of deep sadness for our family because we did not know if he would return home whole or if we would ever see him again. Part of everyday was spent in prayer for his safety. Little did we know of the daily danger he faced and the horror that he saw.

There was much rejoicing when mail arrived and through the boy's letters, we knew they were safe. Bill's letters requested that we send him some tapes of the family singing and cookies. He wanted Kool-Aid to help mask the bad taste of the water. Mama wrote Bill a letter every day and enclosed a package of Kool-Aid. Once he returned home, he said he never wanted to drink the stuff again. The family sat around the table and recorded songs and then mailed them to his address in Vietnam. He later told us that the songs didn't encourage him one bit since they were songs such as "If We Never Meet Again," "Will the Circle Be Unbroken," and "In the Sweet Bye and Bye," however, the cookies were quickly eaten by him and his buddies.

Bill decided to surprise Mama with his homecoming. I will always remember her expression and action when she realized he was standing in the doorway. She was washing dishes and couldn't believe it was him come home. She screamed and cried and almost fainted. He felt bad that he caused such a reaction with his surprise but had she known he was coming I am sure the actions would not have been much different.

We were a close-knit family so the rare "leave times" were special to us all. With my brothers being so far away from home, we didn't seem "whole" and therefore every moment was precious.

Every day there was much worry and anticipation. We knew God loved them more than we; therefore, we trusted Him to do what was right. We believed He heard every whispered prayer from the family members on the behalf of these three we loved so dearly.

Words

Words are used every day for communication but there were certain words that best not come out of our mouths or pass through our lips, whether whispered or yelled. We did not use slang words of *any kind* and saying a curse word should never enter our thoughts, much less be spoken. Mama and Daddy did not allow us to use certain words in frustration and anger because they gave the spirit of slang or cursing. They tried to teach us that by monitoring our spirit we could control our words.

If Daddy heard us say, "I betcha" he would ask, "How much?" Of course, we were taught Christians didn't bet on anything. He would again remind us of his pastor saying, "If you aren't going to be betting, why do you say, 'I betcha'?"

I never remember hearing my mother or father use a slang word or a curse word, not one single time. Daddy recently told me that this was one thing that drew him to Mama. He said she never said bad words nor wanted to do so.

One day several of us were sitting at the dining table talking. Buddy looked out the window and said, "That cow looks pregnant!" Mama said in horror, "Buddy!" He asked, "What do you want me to say, 'with cow'?" We all laughed, but Mama didn't like for us to use the word pregnant and reminded us to choose a different one.

She would say, "She is going to have a baby, whether it be animal or human is sufficient."

We were taught our conversation didn't need to bring attention to body parts that were to be covered. Detailed body functions were privately discussed. My parents were adamant that some things were absolutely off limits for group discussion.

Daddy always told us to be careful with our tone and hurtful words. He often said, "Once a word has been said it can never be recovered. We can apologize but the words have done damage to the person to whom they were carelessly said."

To this day, I cringe when I hear certain words or phrases used. I don't like to hear much sarcasm or joking that is aimed at the individual, because there is an underlying spiteful feeling toward the person. I don't curse nor use slang words and don't appreciate them used in my presence. I am thankful for a Mama and Daddy teaching me to be cautious with my speech.

Churches

I was very young and vaguely remember attending the church in "town." I recall one or two dinners there, the Sunday school class, a few services and some strange individuals that would occasionally come through. I remember having church in our home for a while until the "new" church was built in the "valley."

Most of my memories of a church building are from the small building near the old home place. This building was constructed with the blocks from the old church building in town. I remember it being cold in the winter and hot in the summer. Although we had gas heaters for the winter and a huge fan for cooling in the summer, it was often uncomfortable.

I taught my first Sunday school lesson in the small room on the right side of the platform. I had some good times in that room with the children. It was the beginning of the love I still have for teaching Sunday school.

The little church building was the place where Bible quizzing and drills took place. Many memory verses were learned and quoted there.

Numerous ministers came and preached to the small congregation, giving us encouragement and correction. We saw many souls come to know God in a closer relationship.

I cherish the memory of the prayer meetings, revivals and singing practice. In my mind, I can vividly see the prayer meeting where I became so burdened for Bill's soul. It was the first time that I had ever had such an intense burden for anyone. He received the Holy Ghost that night during the service. After deep, agonizing travail there was much rejoicing in the church and in the heavens. A sinner had come home.

I remember the revival when most of the "young people" prayed and were baptized in the creek. I know that Buddy and I were two of them.

The revival service which stands out most in my mind is the one where Buddy received the Holy Ghost. The next day Johnny (who later became my husband) received it at a noon prayer meeting that JW had requested.

They both preached their first sermons on that little platform. The next year they began preaching revivals as a team. I am so thankful for prayer meetings and revivals where lives are changed, souls renewed, and hearts refreshed.

When Johnny and I began to plan our wedding, it was decided that an altar should be built. I will always remember the building project. It was exciting to see some renovations to the building; and of course, having it done for our day made it special. This would be the first held in the little church. The wedding day and the ceremony is a story of its' own.

My son, Greg went to his first church service at the church there in the "valley" when he was eleven days old. The house of God was a great beginning to life.

Fellowship meetings filled the house to capacity and overflow. Great church was had and then a time of food and fellowship.

I don't remember any funerals being held in the building. That was a good thing.

The final service for us as members at the church was one of mixed emotions for our little family of three. We knew God had called us to Enterprise to pastor, yet our hearts were so entwined with the work in DeFuniak Springs. We were excited for the future but sad because we would no longer be intensely involved in the place where our energy, effort and hearts had been poured for so many years.

Prayer Time

Prayer time was a given at our house. There was always the blessing at mealtimes. The evening was never complete without family prayer at bedtime. No matter who might be in the house at bedtime, everyone was expected to participate. We always knelt at chairs and sofas for our evening prayer. Every family member's name was called. Special needs were brought before the Lord in prayer. If a guest was present, his or her name was called.

I remember as a young teenager having girlfriends sleep over. At bedtime, we were expected to stop what we were doing and join in the prayer time. Not knowing what my friends might think, I was always a bit hesitant about involving them in our family routine. The girls would later say they wished their parents had family prayer like mine. The things I took for granted as a normal part of daily life, others would love to have as a part of their home life.

Even now, at Daddy's house, when it comes time for evening prayer, you will find yourself kneeling, hearing family member's names called, needs brought to the Throne, and a prayer said for you. It is a precious time and a privilege to be included.

This is a tradition that my children, Greg and Melissa, heard and participated in while growing up in our home as well. These days the children are grown. Greg is married and continues the practice of family prayer time with his children. I want these little ones to know prayer is a permanent fixture in Papa and Nana's home as well as their great-grandfather's house.

Special needs were brought to God through prayer. Sometimes it was a few words spoken in passing. I recall Mama having a small growth on her face. One day she was walking one direction in the hallway and Daddy the other. Daddy stopped, laid his hand on Mama's cheek and said these simple words, "Lord, heal my darling," then walked outside. A few days later the growth was gone.

As a child, I had enlarged intestines. This caused me major pain and the need to be careful with my eating habits. After a long time of intense pain, I was taken to the doctor. He said that I needed surgery to correct the problem. Daddy asked me if I wanted surgery or Jesus to heal me. I said that I wanted Jesus to heal me. Daddy and Mama prayed for me. I was healed and never had to have the surgery.

There were times I would miss Mama being in the house. After diligently searching, I would begin calling her name and walk outside. If I didn't soon find her, I would walk toward the church that was down the lane and through the pine trees. Many times, this was done anxiously because I thought the rapture had taken place and I was left behind. Sometimes Mama would be returning from her prayer time at the church or I would find her kneeling at the church altar.

I am so thankful for the consistent prayer life my parents daily exemplified. I have no doubt their prayers kept me from scars that would have lasted a lifetime.

The Bibles

The written Word of God was always a large part of my life as a child. Mama and Daddy had their Bibles open most of the time. Daddy could quote long passages of Scripture from memory. This was because he *read* the Word daily and made special effort to hide it in his heart. Memory verses, Bible drills or trivia were a part of our day. We were taught to memorize the Word of God. I remember small, two or three-word verses that we learned, but I will always remember the first long verse that Daddy had me memorize. It was Philippians chapter 4 and verse 8. Now that I am an adult I often wonder if his purpose for me learning this verse had *life lesson* principle intent. It has served me well and is a favorite scripture of mine today.

Wednesdays at Convention in Ocala, Florida, were always Bible Drill and Bible Trivia contest time for the young people. Daddy would drill us throughout the year and many times we came home with the most prizes. He and Mama both loved scripture trivia questions. They would ask questions that required us to get our own Bibles off the shelf and search for the answers.

Of course, one of the greatest uses Daddy had for his Bible was preparation for church services where he would either be teaching or preaching. His Bible always had little pieces of paper with scripture verses or thoughts on a lesson. Daddy loved his Thompson Chain Reference Bibles and had several through the years. I recently found his first study Bible. It was worn and ragged and filled with precious preaching notes and comments.

It was an everyday sight for us to see Mama with her Bible. Most often it was late evening. Things had settled a bit, allowing her time to sit in her rocking chair and spend a few minutes reading before bedtime and prayer. Mama never had a Bible she could call her own until 1970. She purchased one from the evangelist who was preaching the revival where Buddy and Johnny received the Holy Ghost. I wasn't aware of this until I recently found the old Bible with a scrap of paper inside where she had written this information. The Bible was torn, ragged, and falling apart. It was a much-used book, one that showed a love for the Word of God.

If a Table Could Talk, Oh, the Tales It Would Tell

Growing up, the only dining room table I can remember is the big, round one that still sits in my parent's house today. I know it hasn't always been there because it came from my husband's grandfather. How they "inherited" it I don't know. It has seen at least two sets of dining chairs and one new top, but for me it has always been a part of the kitchen.

If this table could talk, oh my, the things it would say and the stories it would tell. It was, and still is, a table of instruction, correction and grace, don't forget the grace—never forget the grace.

The table was a place for the family meals, but before the meal, there was preparation. Many bushels of peas, corn, turnips, tomatoes, okra, and other vegetables were shelled, shucked and washed here. The table saw countless watermelon, cantaloupe, plums, strawberries, and cucumbers cut up for canning, freezing, or eating. There have been many jars of jelly, jam and pickles placed on the table. The meats are too numerous to name, chicken, goat, turtle, deer, and squirrel being a few, and oh yes, the alligator! Mama made the best desserts and there was always a variety waiting for us to enjoy.

The table was seldom set "fancy." Mama never owned "fancy." We never owned china, the plates seldom matched and there were no cloth napkins or tablecloth. What it lacked in fancy it made up in delicious. My mother was the best cook around. Her vegetables, fruits, jellies, and bread were the best anyone could find. No one eating at my parent's table declined an offer to return.

Those invited to sit at the table were as different as night and day. The children, of course, were there. There were six of us most of the time. The older two would come with their spouses and children. As the family grew, the chairs were scooted closer. Daddy's table slogan was "there's always room for one more," so scoot we did! Thankfully, some chose to sit elsewhere.

Often, we had shoplifters sit at the table. My older brother owns a grocery store and another brother was the meat department manager. They would catch the shoplifters, listen to their story and call the police. After the shoplifter got his or her citation, my brothers or Daddy would often bring them home to Mama for a hot, home-cooked, filling meal. They would be made to feel welcome and then sent on their way.

Relatives would come to the table, sometimes for food, but many times for stories and laughter. I still chuckle as I remember some of the many tales told. The uncles had many stories of their escapades as young men. We were all eager to gather around the table when they were near because we knew we would soon be laughing and having a great time.

Dignitaries have dined at our table. City, county, and state officials have eaten my mother's cooking. They were comfortable, and some returned.

Ministers were consistent and welcome guests at the table. These were the best of times; the story telling, the Bible study and the prayer. Many pastors, evangelists, and missionaries have graced our table. Many young men feeling the call to the ministry have eaten not only Mama's cooking but tasted Daddy's insight into God's Word at that round table. My own husband and younger brother were two of these young men. The hours of Bible study done there could never be calculated and recorded. Today, these ministers are scattered across the United States and other parts of the world and it is amazing to think the round table in my parent's home played a role in their ministries.

Among the many things taking place at the table was income tax preparation, I remember all the receipts strewn about. Bills were paid, homework done, drama lines rehearsed, laundry folded, games played, tea parties given, and memory verses were learned here. This table was a place of activity throughout the day and well into the night.

Did I mention instruction? Did I say discipline? The table is where much of this took place. The memory verses were given practical application here. The "talks," the look me in the eye talks as I tell you the errors of your ways, took place at the dining table. I had rather take a whipping than be called to the table for one of these "talks." But I also remember that wrapped around the correction, instruction and discipline was grace. Grace was always shown for wayward behavior as it was corrected.

My favorite table times were the meals and the fun stories. We girls would often help Mama cook and then we would sit around the table for a meal together as a family unit. One good thing about the farm was the abundance of food available. It may not have been what I wanted but there was plenty. Daddy didn't make us sit silently through the meal, he encouraged us to talk and share our day. If we had company, we were quiet because there were stories to be told. I wish I had recorded these tales. I've forgotten so many of them, but I've not forgotten the feeling of good times at the family table, especially mealtimes where there was plenty of food, iced tea, and fellowship.

When it came time to "set the table" there was one thing that always needed moving. Mama and Daddy's Bibles had to be put aside for a while. The table is where they read the Word each evening. Sometimes, throughout the day if time permitted. Daddy sat at the table and Mama sat in a rocking chair nearby. There was always an open Bible somewhere in the house.

If the family table could talk it would speak not only of laughter but of grief, the tears shed, and the fears revealed. It would tell of the letters written to family far away, letters to sons and brothers in war. Letters written to sons in Vietnam, Germany, and Greenland. It would speak of us opening a letter to learn of a past due bill because of poor health or no job available. Letters opened to tell us a loved one had an incurable disease or informing us of the death of a friend or acquaintance. Yes, the table would speak of the good and the bad, the sorrow and the joy. The table would speak about Life.

The table would tell of a nervous young man speaking with a nervous young girl's father; "Could I marry your daughter, sir?" Then it would tell of the father speaking and the young man quietly listening about responsibility and then receiving the father's blessing.

The table would tell you about the beautiful cake displayed, the candles, the dishes, the food served and the friends attending a wedding reception. It would tell you some of the journey those two young people have traveled because some of it took place while sitting at the table. You just need to be quiet, stop and listen, as it is quite a story.

The table would then tell you about another couple, another adventure, and a longer journey. It would tell you details in the life of this couple that it had observed through the years. It would say, "Look at the cake, see the top, the number 50 is there." Then the table would tell you about the cake that held the number 60 and then 65. This would be my mother and father's story. And what a story you would hear. It would be a good one because it was full of love and ended with a "happily ever after."

The table has moved from the old house and dining room that it had graced for over thirty-five years to a new home, with new stories, new people sitting and dining. Yet it has retained the old and the familiar. It has sat in the new alcove with the bay windows for fifteen years now. New chairs have replaced the old, and now tablecloths are used.

Some things have stayed the same. Mama's rocking chair that always sat nearby remains, the Bible for daily reading is still there although Daddy's eyes are too dim to see, but who knows someone may come by and want to read a passage. And the stories, they are still told, the old and the new.

But other changes have taken place these past years. There are no longer places filled by the laughter of the all children, some are dead and gone on to another world. The food is no longer prepared by Mama; she is no longer with us. The activity around the table has slowed. The visitors are not as frequent, the laughter not as loud, but the memories are still as dear.

Don't forget the blessings at mealtime. The table heard these at least three times a day and then again at any snack time. If the table could speak you might be able to hear Mama's blessing, which never changed "*Thank you, Lord, for this food. Bless the hands that prepared it. Bless it to the nourishment of our bodies to go on the strength to do Your will. In Jesus's name, we pray. Amen.*" The voice is silent but when I sit at the table the prayer is heard—it is quietly heard in the depths of my heart.

The clatter of dishes, the scraping of plates and the overturned glasses are not as many or as loud, but you are still welcome to join those at the table. If you come perhaps you will add another story for the table to tell; after all, it is just "table talk." But the things the table would tell are entertaining, precious and lasting in my mind and in my heart.

The evening prayer can still be heard as the chairs are pulled out. You are welcome to join in. You might as well because bedtime requires prayer time. Just ask the Table.

All Grown Up and Leaving the Farm

In 1969, there was a family that moved to DeFuniak Springs. They had originally lived here years before and were returning to their hometown. This was the Bill Padgett family. His father had been my daddy's pastor many years before. Bill's mother still lived here. When they came to visit her, a visit to us was usually included. They were not strangers to our family. They had a teenage son named John that quickly became my brother, Buddy's best friend. John's family and friends called him Johnny.

The next months and years Johnny spent much of his time with my brother on the farm. They would hunt, fish and roam the woods together, ride motorcycles, and get into mischief. Neither of them had yet given their hearts to the Lord.

In June, the summer of 1970, both Buddy and Johnny received the Holy Ghost. I had received the Holy Ghost as a very young girl, but this same summer I rededicated my life to the Lord.

It was shortly after this, on a July Fourth family gathering at my sister's in Ebro, Florida, Johnny and I "noticed" each other for the first time. We were standing near my daddy's car and Johnny kicked sand on my foot. We began a little game of kicking dirt at each other. On the way home, I rode in the back seat with Johnny and Buddy rode up front with Daddy. He soon began to spend time with me, at least including me more with his and Buddy's activities.

Buddy and Johnny began preaching revivals at churches within a radius of thirty minutes to an hour or two driving distance. I would often go with them to these revivals.

We soon became a couple and began "courting." Most of our time was spent at my parent's home. There wasn't much to do in our little town and money was scarce. Johnny liked my mother's cooking and preferred to eat at my house. We did go to the Tasty Freeze or The Parkway, the only places to get a hamburger, several times throughout the year.

The summer of 1971 Johnny's parents felt led to start a home missions work in Chattahoochee, Florida. Johnny did not feel this was what God wanted for his ministry. Due to this move, we decided to get married a bit sooner than planned.

Johnny asked my daddy's permission for marriage. I do not remember the exact date. We set our wedding date for December 17, 1971. We were young but ready to begin life together! Little did we know what challenges life would bring. But we were in love and that is all that mattered.

We began planning our wedding. Mama spent many hours sewing my wedding dress and bridesmaid's dresses. Flowers were ordered, an organ reserved, and much preparation was made for our special day.

Friends and relatives met for rehearsal Thursday evening. Parts were practiced until everyone was familiar with the program. My daddy said he did not need to practice his part because he had performed weddings many times. After rehearsal, we went to my parent's house for a rehearsal meal Mama had prepared.

The day of our wedding was a busy and much traveled one. The cake was delivered and set up at my parent's house. Because relatives were giving us a break in the expense of several things, Johnny and his mother spent a good portion of the morning driving to Chattahoochee. The one hundred and sixty-mile trip was to pick up the flowers and decorations for the church and reception. After unloading this, he then drove another forty-five minutes one-way to rent an organ. The church did not have one and I wanted organ music for my wedding. Johnny left the organ at the church and quickly drove home to get dressed for the wedding. He was exhausted and was running late. His cousin offered to drive him to the church in his Volkswagen car. On the drive, his cousin said, "Uh-oh, I'm showing empty on fuel."

Johnny said, "Put it on the reserve tank." His cousin said, "I've already used it and forgot to refill." They prayed they would not run out of fuel before they arrived for the wedding. Johnny had scarcely gotten inside the church door when Daddy said, "Let's go."

My daddy walked me down the aisle and gave my hand to Johnny and took over the rest of the ceremony. Daddy may have "performed" many weddings in his lifetime, but this was the first for any of his daughters. He mixed up his lines, forgot the prayer and had Johnny so confused he didn't know his own name, nor did he say, "I do." I was nudging Johnny and said, "Say I do." Daddy heard me and kept going. This has been a teasing point the rest of our lives, Daddy "needing no practice," and us asking if we were truly married since Johnny had not said "I do." I think we are, since they gave us a signed marriage certificate. Elder J. T. Bass spoke up at the end of the ceremony and said, "Well, they are just as married as if it had been done right!"

We left the church and walked down the lane through the pines to the house for the reception. The cake was gorgeous. The table decorations were beautiful, and the reception was fun for all.

Following the reception, as we prepared to leave, the guys "kidnapped" Johnny and the girls "kidnapped" me. They drove us around town and down some dirt roads, in separate cars of course. They returned us to my parent's house about an hour later. We had borrowed Johnny's grandmother's car (he had hidden his) and went to our house to begin our life as newlyweds.

I was grown up now and had a house of my own to tend. I had a husband to take care of and needed to make the house into a home. I continued to return to the farm often; almost every day. I would help in the gardens, putting up the vegetables, butchering the livestock, cleaning the house and "fixing" Mama's hair. Mama and I spent many hours in the kitchen baking for fundraisers for the church.

I still loved the farm. Johnny and I spent much time there, especially on Sunday afternoons for dinner after church. This was a time when several of the family members living nearby would gather and eat with Mama and Daddy. But I was no longer living in the house; I was visiting for the day. After all, I was now all grown-up.

Saying Goodbye to the Farm

Mama passed away June 3, 2004. I remember driving down the lane to the house, tears streaming down my face, knowing that Mama would not greet me at the door this time. But Daddy was there, and we had to carry on. For nine years, he maintained the house for family visits. These nine years were filled with good days, and precious memories were made that I will forever cherish

Tuesday, June 25, 2013, caused the need to add this final chapter. Daddy left this world for "the other side." Friday, June 28, 2013, we laid Daddy next to Mama in his final resting place on this earth.

I left the cemetery and went by the house to say "goodbye" to the farm. Oh, the land and the house will still be there, but it will no longer be the same for me. Someone else will live in the house and someone else will till the land. Different furniture will be brought in; the pictures on the walls will be changed, and a new generation will fill it with memories of their own.

Does this mean that I can never go back, never visit the place again? No. But it will no longer be Mama and Daddy's house, filled with their presence and their belongings. For this reason, I stopped by yesterday to fill my heart again with their "presence." As I walked through the house, I took time to touch their meager possessions and reminisce of their origination and purpose. I took a snapshot in my mind of their belongings in the closets and dresser drawers, the pictures hanging on the walls and sitting on the shelves, the layout of the kitchen, living room, bedrooms, bathroom, and utility.

I once again sat on the furniture imagining our conversations. I visualized Mama in her rocking chair and Daddy lying on the floor in pain as I had seen him so many times.

I visited the pond where many memories were made with Daddy and the grandchildren. I stopped by the old shed out back that held the tools and fishing poles.

The round table was once again used for sharing memories. Instead of my parents and siblings sitting there, it was my children and grandchildren looking through the photo albums as I shared stories of my childhood. I was making new memories with them as I was filling the hole in my heart left by the absence of my parents.

I didn't say goodbye to the lessons learned on the farm. I have taken them with me. They will always be a part of me; therefore, my parents and the farm will live forever in my heart. These lessons are a part of my legacy and heritage to be passed to the future generations.

HONED BY LIFE
PART ONE

Lessons Learned
from the Farm

LIFE LESSONS LEARNED FROM THE FARM

*M*any of these thoughts were written while visiting with my daddy at the farm after my mother passed away. I wish I had taken the time to talk more about life with my mother. I cannot go back, but I can remember the things she did tell, teach, and instill in me.

I spent many days writing my thoughts while watching Daddy sleep. It was time spent, talking, listening and learning and I will never forget them. Yet there was a bit of sorrow because I knew his days left with us were few. As we talked, I saw how much the life lessons from the farm has gone with me into my adult world. These lessons had become the strong foundation of life. Little by little and day by day I had built upon them to become the person I am today. My heart is full of thankfulness to have had the privilege to have the love and influence of my dear parents.

Mama's Enduring Faith

Not many weeks before my mother passed from this life she was in a Pensacola, Florida, hospital. The day she was to be released to go home she fell and broke her hip. We knew this was not good news at her age. Yet Mama's faith was strong. She remained positive even in this setback. Her confidence was in God, he would see her through whatever the outcome. Her hand was still held by a God that had been faithful during their seventy-two years of walking together. She knew that He wouldn't forsake her now.

When I was at the hospital taking care of her after the hip surgery, she had become so weak she could hardly hold her head up
much less put words together. But she would not eat before saying
the blessing. Most of the family could probably quote her blessing; it
has been the same all my life. It was not just a recitation, but a prayer
of thankfulness to God. She was so weak and had to start over four
times before getting it correct. I could have prayed the words for her,
but she needed and desired to do it. Although unable to feed herself,
she made sure the blessing was said.

Mama was sent to rehabilitation therapy at the nursing home in
DeFuniak Springs, Florida. I went down for a visit on her birthday.

The nursing home was awful. I was very distressed as I went
inside. The smell was terrible, and the halls were lined with moaning,
groaning people. I told Mama, "Don't you get depressed, we will not
leave you in here any longer than it takes to get you well enough to
move without causing pain."

She replied, "Please pray that I won't." Believe me I prayed.
That day I talked about everything I could think about to keep her
mind off her surroundings. I told her she needed her glasses, so she
could read. She said, "I don't want to get too spread out and have to
hunt up things when I get out of here." Faith was speaking.

After I had visited Mama a while, Daddy told me he wanted
me to take him into town. He bought Mama a robe, a duster (as she
called it). When he brought it back, he told her "Happy birthday"
then went over to a chair in the corner of the room and took a nap.

While he slept, I asked Mama, "What does Daddy mean to
you?"

She replied, "He is my *everything*." She then gave me a little
story. "A couple of years ago, at Christmas, we decided to not get
each other anything. We really didn't have the money and I didn't
feel like going anywhere to shop, and there was nothing we either
one really needed. So I had it settled in my mind that this was the
way it was to be. On Christmas morning, he had gotten me a black
housecoat. My feelings were kind of hurt. I didn't have anything for
him because we had decided to not get each other a gift.

As she was telling me this, I began to realize she was feeling bad because Daddy had gotten her something for her birthday and she had no way of getting him anything for his that was taking place the next day. I asked, "Mama, do you want me to go buy something for you to give Daddy?"

She looked so sad and said, "I don't have any money."

I said, "Mama, I have some money."

She was lying in the bed and cupped her hands out and said, "Will you share?" To tell you the truth I would have given her every penny I owned at that moment! I said, "I'm not rich but I have enough to get you a gift for Daddy." We talked about what to get him and decided on a neck pillow; since he slept in a chair most of his visits with her. I went to Walmart and got the pillow and chose a birthday card for her to give him. When I returned, Daddy had gone home for a while. She signed the card and we hid the gift behind her oxygen tank. Daddy was surprised the next day when she gave him a gift.

I will always be thankful I could give her a little birthday party that evening. She felt so bad and did not feel like getting out of bed. She made the effort to celebrate and seemed to enjoy herself with a few family members and the nursing staff. I know she enjoyed her cake because she ate every bite that was on her plate. I read her the cards and letters the family had written and compiled into a booklet for her special day, which she enjoyed so much.

Mama was a prayer warrior. Even in the nursing home she was concerned about those around her. The lady sharing her room was in a lot of pain and often called out for help. Mama prayed for her every time the lady cried out. In her own pain, she continued to ask God to help others.

Not many days after her birthday we had to take her back to the hospital. My last recollection of her praying was on Saturday, May 31. Johnny and I had been to Mississippi and on our way home we stopped by the hospital in Pensacola. She was so feeble, but when she saw Johnny with me, she kind of sat up in the bed. Her voice was weak, but I understood enough to know she wanted him to pray with her. I asked, "Mama, do you want us to pray with you?" She said, "That was what I was trying to say." I will never forget that frail little body, lifting her hands as high as possible from her sides, closing her eyes and praying through the oxygen mask. She praised God and told him of her love for him, never asking him to heal her; she simply thanked him for his love. After Bill, Johnny and I stopped praying she continued for a while. This is my last memory of her praying, but one I will always cherish.

I will miss Mama's prayers. Had it not been for her faithful prayers I don't know where I would be today. She prayed for me every day of my life. I knew I could call and ask her to pray, or if I told her of a need or a burden it would soon be taken before the Throne. I had experience with her enduring faith and knew that God heard and answered Mama's prayers.

I hope hearing my voice lifted in prayer remains a common occurrence for my children and they too have the assurance I will bring them before the throne every day. My goal is to have for myself the same enduring faith as my mother.

The last few months of Mama's life I tried to go down at least once a week and clean the house, bathe her and wash her hair. I am thankful to have lived near enough to do this for my mother. The last time I fixed her hair she was so weak that she was unable to hold her head straight. I finally quit telling her to hold her head up and just moved it back into position. She loved to look pretty and taught us girls to always look our best. The last Saturday in the hospital, as I brushed her hair up a bit she said, "My hair is so dirty and needs fixing." I told her I would try to find some dry shampoo and take care of it. Unfortunately, I was not able to do so. I will miss fixing her hair so much; I did it for many years and never felt it a duty but a privilege. She was so appreciative. Daddy was thankful and enjoyed that his girls made sure Mama looked pretty for him. Ellen, Judy, and I made sure she looked beautiful for her homegoing service.

I will never, never forget those last couple of days in the Pensacola hospital. The times the family sang and prayed together around her bedside. It was precious to me and will be a forever cherished memory. There was such a sweet presence of God. What a way to go from this life into the everlasting!

I am thankful that my children, Greg and Melissa, could visit Mama in the hospital and have a bit of interaction those last days. She was so excited when Greg and Kimberly came by to tell her they were going to have their first child. Melissa lived out of state and had not had much time with her grandmother in recent months. She had so much wanted to speak with her, but Mama had "drifted" away from us. As Melissa was preparing to leave for home, she went to the bedside to tell her granny goodbye and that she loved her. Melissa knew her grandmother had spent much time in prayer especially for her. Mama had not had any interaction for a couple of days and when Melissa spoke, she opened her eyes and tried to focus; it was a precious moment spent together. Mama left this life as Melissa was driving into Nashville. She later called and said, "Mama, you can put in Granny's book, 'Granny, we will miss your cooking, your love and you, but we *know* where to find you."

That is the joy of Mama's homegoing; we know where to find her. It is my prayer that each of my family continues to carry the godly heritage that Mama gave us on into the next generations. I want to be with her in eternity. Heaven is sounding sweeter all the time.

I thank God for a wonderful mother, a mother of enduring faith (June 2004).

Daddy's Guidance for Living Life

Influence is "the capacity to have an effect on the character, development, or behavior of someone or something, or the effect itself."

Daddy was one of the greatest influences of my life. His guidance and leadership were based upon the Word of God. His daily example left a lifetime of inspiration.

Principle, strong beliefs and moral values were Daddy's foundation. A principle is a standard of moral or ethical decision-making. Since the Bible was his compass for life, he felt it was a book that held the key to instruction for living holy and dying triumphantly.

From early childhood God was at the center of our home, jobs, family, and friends. Daddy's employers knew he was a man bent on pleasing God. Our unsaved family knew that church attendance was more important to him than a Sunday social call. They knew to wait until after we returned home to visit. His friends were chosen carefully.

Daddy said there is a difference between a woman and a lady. A lady doesn't draw unnecessary attention to herself by boisterous behavior. He taught me that I could attract the positive or the negative through the way I dressed, the way I talked and the content of my conversation, my behavior and even my posture.

The little poem, "The wise old owl sat in the oak, the more he heard the less he spoke, the less he spoke the more he heard, why can't we be like that wise old bird?" was often quoted in our home. I think it was his way of telling me there was a time to be quiet and a time to speak.

Daddy taught me by example that at times you must keep going when the body aches and you want to quit and you're wondering if the effort is worth it all. Daddy said the pleasure felt from a completed task would be worth the effort, energy, and time spent.

My daddy believed everything we read, hear and see has an impact on the development of who we become. Our character traits, choices in life and our eternal destination are contingent upon these things.

Daddy's effect on my behavior patterns and character development weren't realized until many years down the road from my days under his authority. I am so appreciative of his instructions and have found them a wealth of knowledge I can go to even though he is no longer around.

Observing, listening and still learning as we spent his last days on earth together, I realized the greatest lesson Daddy taught me was not only how to live, but how to die. He was a great teacher (June 2014).

On Being a Lady

I was a girl bent toward being outside enjoying the noisy and rambunctious activities with my brothers. This presented a challenge to my parents in their efforts to train me to become a lady. In my development from childhood to womanhood Mama and Daddy wanted me to become a lady in all areas of life.

I was to bend at the knees, not the waist. I was told to keep my knees together when sitting and my legs crossed at the ankles. Do not slurp or burp in public. Keep your arms and elbows off the table, take little bites, chew quietly, and don't talk with food in your mouth. Keep your feet and your chair on the floor. Don't slump, slouch, flop, or wallow; sit straight and stand tall.

Daddy believed in laughter, lots of laughter. But a lady wasn't boisterous, demanding, or silly—bringing attention to herself.

My clothing was to be clean and pressed. I should never expose or bring attention to parts of my body through my choice of attire. My knees should always be covered.

My conversation was to be about ideas, not people. I was to never talk about private matters of the family. There were parts and functions of the body that were to never be discussed in mixed company and a lady should always blush when it occurred.

Mama said, "Be good, learn to be good."

It is my hopes that I have made them proud and have the reputation of a lady.

Hospitality

Growing up we didn't have fancy. We didn't have much by this world's description of wealth. What we had was an abundance of love, friendship, and fellowship to offer. Our home was one of open heart, open home. Friends were embraced. Strangers were welcome and soon became friends. My parents believed in the scriptural teachings that we are to be "lovers of hospitality."

Our doors were never locked. In the world in which we live today this is a rarity. But our doors were always open day or night. Out of town friends and relatives traveling through knew there was always a bed awaiting them if it was needed.

Often, in the middle of the night a friend would come in the house and Daddy would say, "Who is it?" The person would identify themselves and Daddy would reply, "You know where your room is, we will see you in the morning."

I remember a young evangelist was traveling with his new bride and needed a place to stop for the night. He told his wife, "I know where we can stay. Bro Adkison lives a few miles from here, we will go there for the night."

She said, "Don't we need to call and make sure that it is okay for us to come."

He said, "No, it will be fine." When they arrived, he got their suitcase out of the car and told her to come with him. As they walked into the house. Daddy heard them and asked, "Who is it?" The evangelist told him who they were, and Daddy responded with his usual words, "You know where your room is, we will see you in the morning." The young wife could not believe what had just happened. But she knew from thereon there was a room and a bed awaiting them if they needed it while traveling through our town.

In these times I am not like my parents with the unlocked doors allowing just anyone to walk into my home, but I have opened my home to countless people through the years. We have hosted friends, relatives, missionaries, and folks that needed somewhere to stay for a few days while getting settled into a new home. And like my parents' house, my house was not completed for many years. The house was not the reason they came; it was the feeling of "home" that they encountered.

Like my parents, we have had wall-to-wall children sleeping on the floor. We have had many evenings of laughter, staying up until the early hours of the morning telling stories and having a great time making memories. These times were so much like those of my growing up years and I am thankful my children could experience them. It is times like these that lodge in our hearts and remain dear to us these many years later.

Mama always had food to serve. It might not be gourmet, but it was delicious when shared with company. It might be breakfast at night, a sandwich and a glass of tea or a simple cake. Through this I learned to always keep something quick to prepare in case we had "drop in" guests. These types of guests are the reason I have a "Company Vegetable Soup" recipe today.

On one occasion, we had unexpected guests needing to be fed and I didn't know what to prepare. I had some ground beef, some cans of vegetables, and a can of tomato juice. I threw it all in a pot and let it cook while I made some grilled cheese sandwiches. I added some Dorito chips to our plates to complete the meal. This became one of our favorite "after-church" meals for many preachers and their families when in our home.

Mama taught me, "use what you have and act like it is the best and folks will think it so." She was right! And like my parents' home, our guests return again and again.

Some Things in Life Are a Given

The question, "Are we going to church today?" was never heard in our home. Church attendance and involvement was a given. If the doors were open and something happening, we were there. It didn't matter whether it be worship, outreach, or workdays, we were there. No ifs or buts, we were there. Living on a farm we were always tired, so tiredness was never an excuse. Sickness was a possible reason to stay home, but only if the requirements were met. We had to have a contagious disease, throwing up, high fevers and pretty much flat on our backs to be exempt from church attendance. Feeling weary, depressed, angry, or pouting was the decisive motivation to be in the Lord's house. My parents felt this was a time to arrive early for prayer and allow opportunity for a change of heart and mind, attitude and behavior. We were taught needs would be met; miracles could happen, souls saved, and lives changed in the house of God. Mama and Daddy always expected Jesus to show up, knowing when he did great and mighty things took place. And they did.

My parents taught us the questions of life could be answered through hearing the preached Word, but you had to be in church for it to be beneficial.

As previously stated, growing up in my parents' home meant church attendance. It was not only attending church at our local assembly, but Daddy would take us to churches in the area on nights we didn't have a service. We would get home from school, do our homework, quickly eat, dress for church, and then drive anywhere from thirty minutes to two hours for a service. We would arrive home late at night and at times it was the early hours of the morning. We were expected to get up and be at school the next day and most likely do the same thing with church that evening. Revivals in those days were seven nights a week and often lasted several weeks. By the way, I had perfect school attendance from the sixth grade until my senior year. Late nights at church didn't hinder school attendance or my grades.

I didn't always want to be at church and do all this traveling. There were many times I had rather be at home reading a book or sleeping. But it wasn't up to me. My parents left no option but to be ready to go when the time came.

Today, I am thankful my parents took me to church and involved me in the work of God. This gave clear direction for my life as a saint of God, a pastor's wife, and an example to my children. *"I was glad when they said unto me, Let us go into the house of the LORD."*

Influence

We always had a dog hanging around the farm. Some were for hunting birds or hogs, but many of our dogs were pets. Whenever we had a dog that would get into our chicken coop, Daddy said he would have to get rid of the dog. He said once it has gotten "blood in his teeth" it would cause trouble from there on. I remember begging Daddy to not do away with one of my favorites. He sat me down and gave me a life lesson about the "taste of blood" and its damage.

While spending time at the farm recently, I began to think on this danger. I've watched people get a 'taste for blood' as discontentment crept into their lives. They quickly became dissatisfied with their spouse, their preacher, their employer and their friends. We must guard our heart and not allow this to happen, whether it come from our own discontentment or allowing others to transfer their dissatisfaction to us. The wisdom of scripture gives us specific instruction on how to deal with this attitude. *"And have no fellowship with their unfruitful work of darkness, but rather reprove them"* (Ephesians 5:11). We are to be careful of the voices that influence our lives.

Correction with Love

There is much truth in the statement, "You will reap what you sow." Recently, reminiscing at the old farm place, I remembered my daddy giving my brother, Buddy and me the job of planting corn. The ground had been prepared, the seed handed to us and instructions given. Daddy left us and went to work in another field. We worked, laughed, fussed and finally got tired of planting the row after row of corn. We decided to dig a hole and bury the rest of the seed and head home. Arriving home, Daddy commented on how quickly we had gotten the job done. I don't recall our answer but nothing else was said. Several weeks later Daddy took us to the field and showed us the yield of our labor. There was a nice stand of corn growing, all in one place. He knew what we had done (probably the day we did it). But this day we got a life lesson on our "sins finding us out" and "reaping what we had sown." Daddy didn't spank us, but we did get a "talking to" about trust, waste and cost. He explained that he had trusted us to do a job, but we had wasted precious seed. When sprouting so closely the corn would not produce; therefore, causing unnecessary expense and lack of productive income. My memory says there were several Scriptures quoted during this lesson; "reaping what you sow," "your sins finding you out," "wastefulness," "slothfulness," and "the ant is wise, but the sluggard will have nothing in the harvest"…I know these were among those quoted. And of course, included was the "you had best never do this again" talk. This lesson of my wrong, never completely covered, has stayed with me through the years.

Another valuable lesson was learned through this. Although we had done wrong, Daddy still loved us, we were his children. He was firm in correction, but not abusive, mercy was shown as he gave us instruction on the necessity of being wise with both time and substance. He desired us to become good and productive citizens.

What a lesson! My heavenly Father has loved me even in my times of deliberately doing wrong. His love is unconditional. His love corrects me yet expects me to learn from my mistakes. When this correction is accepted, I become profitable for His kingdom.

I think it has done me good to visit the old farm place and revisit some of those "life lessons" my daddy taught me as a youngster.

A Time to Work and a Time to Rest

My daddy believed in hard work. He had no tolerance for laziness. He worked tirelessly and taught us to do our best in everything.

Growing up on the farm the days were busy, from dawn to well into the evening hours. There was always ground to till, seed to plant, gardens to hoe and vegetables to be harvested. Those same vegetables were then prepared for the buyer, "put up" in the freezer or canned. There were blueberries, strawberries, plums, and watermelon in season.

Daddy believed in every family member doing his or her share of the work. I would get so tired of harvesting the produce, shelling the peas, husking the corn, washing turnips, and on and on. Added to this was the care of the animals, and then slaughter days. Mama also expected help with the housework. Work, work, work... I could sure do some complaining as a child and teenager.

But looking back, it wasn't all work. We had playtime. Each day in the summer we would have an hour to swim in the creek. We had time to play games of make believe and build castles in the pine straw. A favorite time was the opportunity to lay in the yard with Daddy and see creation in the clouds by day and gaze at the stars by night. There was time for reading books, lengthy talks at the table, and even an occasional visit to the beach. There was time for Scripture discussion and visits with family and friends.

No, it wasn't all work. No, it wasn't too bad growing up on the farm, where there was plenty to eat, lots of love for everyone and life lessons woven into each day. I look back and realize I had a blessed life.

The lessons of working hard, getting chores completed, spending time in relaxation for the body and setting aside time for visits with our Savior are worthy to be passed on to the next generation. These lessons learned from the farm will always be a part of who I am.

Some Things Are Not for Sale

My parents purchased my mother's "home place" right after I was born. It was a one hundred sixty-acre plot of land. Mama and Daddy worked hard to pay for this property. They tilled the soil long before I was old enough to help. I could run, play, and enjoy the wide-open fields while they worked to plant gardens and trees.

The day came when I was old enough to help with what needed to be done on the farmland. Many days and years of early rising to help plant, pick, and store the crops were now my daily routine. I became a "part" of the land, investing time, energy and love into the "home place" that now meant so much to me.

Several years ago, I was called for jury duty. The case was the City of Enterprise, Alabama versus an elderly couple. The city wanted to expand the local airport. They needed this couple's land to do so. When my name was called, I was asked if I knew the couple. I replied, "No, I don't, but I have seen them around town." The lawyer then asked me if I knew what the case was about and made a statement that allowed me to express my feelings concerning the situation. I replied, "Yes, sir, I do." I then proceeded to inform them that some things cannot be bought because they aren't for sale, at any price. I then explained that my parents owned land that had been in our family for many years and generations. I said while other land *could* be purchased it would not be the same as the land that was passed from generation to generation because these held personal investment and memories. I then went on to say, "Actually, the Bible gives an account of something similar in the story of Naboth's vineyard." When I spoke these words, the entire courtroom turned to stare at me in amazement (or horror). Yet I continued and said, "His land wasn't for sale." The lawyer kind of smiled and said, "Thank you, you may be seated."

I came home and told my husband what had taken place. He was a bit astonished that I would be so bold. He just looked at me and said, "You actually said that?" I said, "Yes, I did. I was on the back row of the courtroom and was wishing the floor would open and swallow me when the entire courtroom turned and stared, but I stated my feelings. They shouldn't have asked!"

It may not have been the proper response for a jury selection but something inside of me rose in defense of this couple. They were elderly, the land had been theirs for years, their children had been raised there, memories were everywhere and besides they did not wish to sell.

That evening at church a lady came up and said, "I heard you caused an interesting jury selection today." Her dad had been in the crowd for jury selection also and had told her what had taken place. I said, "I guess he also told you I wasn't selected for that trial."

My parents instilled within me the value of ownership for things and the worth of humankind. They showed by example how to work hard and then enjoy the fruit of my labor. I appreciate these lessons; their influence caused my opposition to the City taking this couple's property.

I did not follow the trial, but the airport was expanded. The City either found other land nearby to purchase or reached an agreement with this couple. I hope the elderly couple remembers they had at least one person on their side in the courtroom that day. It was definitely a day I will remember...*and it all began on the farm!*

The Need for Boundaries

Years ago, I attended a conference for home school parents. One of the classes focused on boundaries. While sitting there I had a profound understanding of the need for boundaries. I also listened as the instructor talked about my childhood and how determined I was to move those boundaries established by my parents. She spoke of how I would try one boundary, discovering it was stable and immoveable. She told how I would go to the next and learn it was secure. Then I would go to the next. She wasn't really talking about me, but the basic tendencies of humanity, yet it was exactly what I had done as a child. I left the session with a better understanding of my parents' purpose for defining lines, a knowledge of my children's tactics of boundary removal and I was better equipped to understand the drive of my students.

The definition of boundary is: The official line that divides one area from another, limits, or restrictions.

Boundaries. Limits. Restriction. Those were not the words I wanted to hear while growing up on the farm. It was those limits and restrictions my parents believed in setting that caused me to question and often push and shove. The struggle was real.

Mama and Daddy understood setting boundaries was not an option. My young mind could not grasp their reasoning, but that didn't matter, their goal was to protect me from battles I was not yet mentally, physical or spiritually prepared to face.

Mama and Daddy were wise in knowing they had God-given parental responsibilities that had to be administered. In their wisdom they understood they couldn't "let it go" this time. My parents wanted lasting effect, something to carry me through the journey of life. Mama and Daddy realized boundaries were necessary for our household. Defining, lines had to be drawn and they were the ones qualified to do the drawing, not the children.

They were the parents. Children need their parents to guide, lead and develop them into mature and productive adults. My parents knew there was safety in restriction. They had parents that had taught them the importance of drawing definite lines. They had experience and knowledge of the fact that as children we don't know how to face the adversity of a godless society.

Being a strong-willed child, I many times asked the question, "Why?" I wanted a different answer than the one given. If I could provoke enough, I just might be able to get them to budge a bit. But being wise, and having been children themselves my parents understood the need to stand firm.

Compromising or conceding to the pressure of a slowly maturing young girl would have long term damaging effect. Mama and Daddy understood this and stayed firm. By them not giving in to my tears and sometimes harsh words, I was not only kept from many dangers and wrong decisions, I discovered the security that every individual needs to possess. As maturity came, I saw my parents' decisions offered safety, security and stability. I learned to respect and value the boundaries set in my life. At times, I literally tremble to think how life could have turned out so different had I not been willing to listen and learn. Thank you, Mama and Daddy, for providing this lesson, enabling me to choose well, instead of living a life of regret. Your boundaries have served and fulfilled their intended purpose.

Telling the Truth and the Importance of Integrity

The preacher talked about heaven and hell. I didn't want to go to hell. "Liars don't go to heaven," he said. When I was caught in a lie Mama and Daddy would ask, "Honey, do you want to go to heaven?"

The Bible teaches that all men (and women) are liars. Ever since the Garden deceit has been in existence. Lies are told for various reasons, all resulting in bad consequence.

The definition of a lie: a false statement made with deliberate intent to deceive; intentionally giving a false impression. Misrepresentation in any form is not truth. Anything not true is a lie. "*Thou shalt not bear false witness against thy neighbor*" (Exodus 21:16).

Daddy told me about a young woman that became angry and disgruntled at a church. She falsely accused her preacher of a moral wrongdoing. He had no way in which to "prove" her accusations false. It was many years later that she confessed to not being truthful.

But damage had been done. The man's integrity had been questioned and his ministry tarnished.

"*Lying lips are an abomination to the Lord*" (Proverbs 12:22). Abomination is extreme hatred. "*God hates a lying tongue*" (Proverbs 6:17). Lying has consequence in God's eyes. "*No one who practices deceit shall dwell in my house...*" (Psalm 101:7). Speaking truth is vital to every individual's character, whether it be the person speaking or the person spoken about. God is angry when a person lies and destroys another's reputation.

A person's integrity is to be valued and protected. Integrity is defined as *soundness of moral and ethical character, honesty.* God is serious about our treatment of others. "*A false witness will not go unpunished, and he who breathes out lies will perish*" (Proverbs 19:9).

Mama and Daddy taught us lying is a sin. They taught that a lie was a lie. They said there was no such thing as a black lie or a white lie; a lie was and is a lie and will always be a lie. Even when joking, truth must be spoken. The word truth means: *the actual state of a matter, a verified or indisputable fact; conformity with fact or reality.*

Before Daddy and Mama were married, he told her to never call him a liar. He said he might get his information a little wrong, but not intentionally, and if this was the case, she could correct him once they had gotten home.

Like Mama and Daddy, I might get my information mixed up from time to time and need correcting, but I will not intentionally lie or try to deceive. After all, Mama and Daddy taught me to tell the truth and to always guard my integrity.

Aborted Aspirations, Fulfilled Desires

As a youngster, I had an interest in solving mysteries. This came from growing up reading Nancy Drew, The Boxcar Twins and Hardy Boys books. I wanted to become either a detective or a lawyer.

During one of my junior high years my daddy was called to jury duty for a murder trial. This caught my attention for several reasons; Daddy had to be sequestered for the length of the trial, a local citizen had been killed, and I had a lot of "knowledge" about this kind of thing due to my extensive "mystery" readings.

This was an often-discussed topic for several weeks following the trial. The murder and subsequent trial were published in a detective magazine, which Daddy bought and brought home for us to read. With my interest in mysteries and detective stories, I read every case in the magazine. Here began my curiosity in forensic science, along with the way a lawyer presents the prosecution and defense. I decided I wanted to become a prosecuting attorney.

Throughout the next few years I read many detective magazines and books that involved solving murders and the prosecution of the murderers. My brother owned a grocery store, and this enabled me to have detective magazines on hand at any time.

Yet solving murders and court representation was not what God had planned for my future. He knew I would not be able to work in these fields of labor and serve Him as He desired and planned.

> *For I know the thoughts and plans that I have for you, says the Lord, thoughts and plans for welfare and peace and not for evil, to give you hope in your final outcome.* (Jeremiah 29:11, AMP)

Although God led my life in a different direction than my youthful aspirations, he has allowed me to have contact with both the workings of the law and forensic science. I was privileged to see firsthand how the field of forensic science works. I personally met the artist that drew the sketch making it possible for the arrest of one of the top ten "Most Wanted" in the United States. I asked her many questions about the process of solving a case. I was able to observe the way dental work, scattered bones, an autopsy, fingerprints, and profile drawings were used in solving a crime. It wasn't a sin for me to have an interest in these areas; God just wanted me to serve in another capacity. I am thankful God knows what I need. "Happy is that people whose God is the Lord."

The Box

People are naturally curious. Curious people want "details." When they can't get "the scoop" they tend to jump to conclusions without the knowledge of fact. First Timothy 6:4 warns us to separate ourselves from those fond of constant questioning and "evil surmising." The word surmise means: *an idea or opinion based on insufficient conclusive evidence; to make a guess or conjecture; supposition, imagine, speculate.* So "evil surmising" is wrongful and sinful supposition and speculation about another with insufficient evidence.

One evening Daddy asked me to sit at the table with him. I knew *this time* I had done nothing in which to be disciplined, so I wondered, "What?"

He said, "Honey, some of the children on the bus are asking me why you won't allow them to look in the box you carry every day; they wonder what is in it." The "box" that Daddy was questioning me about was a cigar box I had gotten from somewhere and prettied it a bit with artwork. I told my daddy, "There is nothing important in the box, but it is MY box and it is no one's business what it holds." I went and got my box and showed him the contents, which was bits of paper, pencils, odds and ends that little girls collect, and a couple of pictures of friends and family. Daddy looked at the contents and smiled. He then handed me the box and said, "Okay, if they ask again, I will tell them they will need to find out from you because I won't tell." I will never forget my mother (she was in the kitchen paying close attention to our conversation) and Daddy understanding the importance of my box. They didn't make fun of me but regarded this as my personal property and allowed me to reveal the contents whenever I was ready. When I finally allowed friends to look in my box, most were very disappointed by what they found. In their minds, they "knew" I had some spectacular item inside that little box. No, it held nothing either awe-inspiring nor bad, it was just my box, and no one had a need to know its content.

Curiosity has the capability to cause much embarrassment, a lot of backtracking and the need to apologize. It pays to be slow in judgement and remember there are times the reality of a situation isn't always as it seems.

As the wife of a pastor and sitting with him in counseling I have been privy to other people's affairs. Each incident was private and deserved my silence concerning its disclosure. Few people confide their true feelings. It is important that I handle these confidences with carefulness and discretion.

Other's "boxes" may be prettied up as mine was, or maybe not. We may never know the contents. Until we do, we cannot be the judge and jury.

When my "box" is the next one on the table being examined and scrutinized, I would desire those that question and examine my case handle it with carefulness, reigning in their curiosity and surmising, because as I previously stated; things aren't always as they seem.

Time Brings Change

I am at the farm today and feeling a bit melancholy at change. I don't like the uneasiness of the unknown that change brings. Change demands letting go of the old to receive the new. Although necessary, I find it painful. Yet I know if change had not taken place, there would be no growth and development. I would remain at home, never attending school, never have gotten married and matured. It was change that brought the joy of children and grandchildren of my own. I understand things can't and won't remain the same; yet I am still saddened by changes that have happened too quickly.

I took a walk today while at the farm and was overwhelmed with memories and a feeling of loss. The home and house of my childhood are gone. The family unit as I knew it no longer exists. Mama, three siblings and several in-laws are no longer with us. I don't like those changes. The house no longer stands where I spent my childhood. The land stands vacant, void of block, concrete, lumber, glass, shingle and nail. I can no longer go to my bedroom and enjoy the days of playing with my brother and sleeping with my sisters. I can no longer sit at the desk where I did homework and wrote letters to friends, and notes to my parents. The kitchen Mama occupied for years, is gone. The stove no longer holds leftovers for children that might "just drop by." Gone is the back porch where many activities were held, everything from pea shelling, corn husking, hog slaughtering, family reunion meals, great drama entertainment and grandchildren cutting "records." The trees no longer stand, swaying in the wind, offering shade for the weary hot farmhand and plenty of pine straw for forts, egg hunts and strawberry bedding. They have been cut and young ones planted. The barn, the smoke house and pump shed still stand, and while they each hold memories, they aren't the house that held the laughter, tears, instruction, and discipline. A new home has been built and while it holds dear memories, it lacks much of the old because I never lived there.

Another change is my daddy. He is an old man now. The man that stood straight and tall is now slump-shouldered, bent by time, labor and life. The mind is still sharp, but the ears not as apt to hear, and the eyes are almost blind. Time has taken away the energetic man that loved to wrestle with the five sons after a hard days' work and "steal" whatever book the three girls might be reading

My siblings and I too have gone through change, some have left this world, dying much too young. The ones remaining, should I mention the hair, once so dark is now grey or gone. Like Daddy, our bodies are moving slower, needing the young family members to take more responsibility. No matter how I try, I am unable to stop these changes.

Change, although needed and unavoidable, is emotionally difficult. Yet God gives strength to go forward and is with me for every step required. I am unable to stop the arrival of a new day as it brings more change, but I can bring the precious memories, the stories of love and laughter and lessons learned from the farm into this new place in life. The new generation needs the sharing of my memories from the farm, their lessons giving hope for the future.

Just another day of thinking while at the farm. (4/4/13)

A Balanced Life

"Let me be weighed in an even balance that
God may know mine integrity." (Job 31:6)

As I sit at the dining table in my parents' house, I see the balance scale in their curio cabinet. It was a gift received on their fiftieth wedding anniversary. I'm not sure if the person giving it realized the importance it played in my parent's everyday life. Theirs was a life of balance.

As I sit and think and cry and write, I have no doubt this was a way of life for them. They lived and taught balance in the family, balance in marriage, and balance with work and play.

Balance was evident in family. Mama and Daddy desired peace and calm in the home; they made sure balance reigned, providing the stability and security we needed.

It was evident my parents not only loved each other but truly enjoyed each other's company. Neither selfishly demanded his or her wants to be met, but always seeking ways to please each other.

While we complained about things not being fair, we knew impartiality was given to each of us. We unsuccessfully tried to trick them into choosing a favorite. When I would ask Daddy if I was his favorite, he would always reply, "You're one of them."

Mama and Daddy expected obedience and good behavior. We were children and didn't always comply, yet the required correction and discipline was done with the balance of love.

In work, Mama and Daddy portrayed balance. A bushel of peas was always pressed down, shaken, and piled high. Blueberry baskets were measured full and running over. The Bible verse that I often heard growing up was Proverbs 11:1: "A false balance is abomination to the LORD; but a just weight is his delight."

Even in working the fields balance was shown. We were allowed play breaks during the day's work. My parents knew this balance of work and rest was needful.

Everything we did was balanced with God's Word. Bible reading and prayer balanced each day at the farm.

Lessons from the farm. (4/13)

On Marriage

Marriage is not a joy ride taken in a sports car with the top down, the wind blowing through the hair and the spirit carefree. It more resembles a cross-country trip. Through the darkness, the dawn breaks forth as we follow the winding road. The skyline is bright with the sun rising over the mountains, bringing hope for a new day. Travelling through the valley the rain falls and a rainbow beams gloriously across the sky giving beauty after the storm. The desert is hot, dry and lonely but ahead a stream offers its cooling refreshment. There is debris in the path hidden by the bend in the road, we can forge ahead or wisely take the time to remove it. There are the needed stops for fuel, food and sustenance. Tomorrow there will be more miles to travel with mountains to climb and rivers to cross. Yet as twilight falls and the day comes to an end, we realize there is joy in the journey, breathtaking views, and bountiful blessings along the way.

Take time to look around at your world. How many marriages can you acknowledge to be great examples? Few have relationships that need to be copied. My grandchildren are observing a generation seeking their own selfish desires. There is no thought to making vows of commitment. The busyness of life, always searching for that job with a bigger income and making sure the children participate in every activity offered doesn't satisfy and fulfill. This pursuit not only encumbers, it keeps couples from having a secure, fruitful, and right relationship with God and each other. Sadly, embracing God first in a marriage is counter-cultural to this world.

I loved hearing about my parent's young, developing love. Their newlywed moments were wonderful and precious. They were mature enough to know they had plenty to learn. It was essential for both to make a lot of changes. A good, successful and fulfilling marriage is hard work and requires conscious effort to do right from both individuals.

Mama and Daddy were not exempt from the human faults. They discovered neither had married the perfect spouse. Are you aware that everyone's definition of "perfect" will be different? And have you observed that at some point every individual displays a bit of selfishness? Being human, my parents had different views at times. They didn't always see eye to eye and I'm sure there was verbal disagreement. Yet I never heard it. They were wise and took any argument away from my ever-hearing ears and always watchful eyes.

Mama and Daddy leaned on the principles and promises from God's Word to guide them in marriage. It is all they needed. They knew if they could get the principles of The Word embedded into their marriage it would be better than any other book or seminar available.

My parents exemplified sacrifice, using Jesus Christ as their example. A definition of sacrifice is surrendering what one values for something one values even more. They took to heart the teaching of God's Word—love God, love your neighbor. This is how they lived; marriage was no longer about their desires, emotions, and feelings, but pleasing their partner for life.

Mama and Daddy knew their children, grandchildren and extended family needed the positive effect a healthy and happy marriage would bring. They were aware it was a process that took time, a long time. They stayed together, worked out their differences and did their very best to create a happy and lasting marriage. I believe they did an awesome job. Sixty-nine and a half years together and still in love wasn't too bad!

Johnny and I were asked to do a marriage retreat, so I decided to go see Mama and Daddy and get them to tell me what they would advise couples concerning marriage. I had read it takes most couples at least ten years to change the way they did things as a family growing up and start building their own way. Mama and Daddy were about to celebrate sixty-two years of marriage, so I felt they were the best source for information. I had watched their marriage first-hand and knew it had worked. The following are selections from what my parents told me in my "interview" with them:

DADDY:

Tell them to just be good to each other all their days.

Always seek to please the other, not wanting everything *your* way.

MAMA:

You won't always see eye to eye but there is a way to get along. You can sweetly and pleasantly talk it out.

Take care of each other in every way. Pay attention to the small details and it will make the marriage great.

Mama advised against using credit cards. In all their years of marriage they never had a credit card. She said if you use one, only charge what you can pay off within thirty days.

To this, Daddy added that he had seen too many marriages break up because of reaching out for too many *things* and not being able to pay, then the pressure causing a breakdown in the marriage. He said to never live beyond your means.

DADDY:

Always agree when dealing with the children. He said he and Mama made the following agreement before they married; "When children come along, when I correct the child you won't say anything, even if you disagree with the way I handle it, when we are by ourselves we will discuss it, and I will do the same for you."

I can truthfully say that they put this into practice. I remember *one* time that Mama interfered when Daddy was correcting me. She thought he was spanking me a little too hard. Of course, I did too. He calmly told her if she couldn't be quiet to please leave the room. She said, "I'm sorry, and left the room." I don't remember the reason I was being corrected, but I do remember what *they did*.

The word treasure means *something very much valued*. As I have observed their relationship through the years, it was evident they valued each other. Daddy made Mama his queen, making it easy for him to be the king of the 'castle.' Theirs was a never-ending circle of trust, love, and respect allowing the other to feel important, treasured, and loved.

Daddy constantly told Mama she was beautiful. When we would have family gatherings, he would put his arms around us girls and tell folks, "I have some beautiful daughters, but they sure can't compare with their mama." This statement didn't make us feel bad; it only reinforced our knowledge of his love for our mother.

I was visiting Mama and Daddy one day not too long before Mama died. She was in bed with a big pot and spoon. I asked her why she had them in bed. She answered, "Your daddy gave me these to bang on when I need to get his attention." I asked her, "Does it work?"

She laughed and said, "I bang and bang and bang before he ever comes to see what I need." I then asked her if she threw it at him when he finally came. She said, "Oh, honey, I wouldn't do that!" And she wouldn't. You must understand Daddy is one of those men that would not sit still. He was going to be out and about, and his hearing was bad. The remedy was to get a wireless doorbell. Mama had one part and Daddy the other. She told me he often forgot to carry his part of the bell with him.

Several years after the first interview I was asked to help Johnny teach another marriage retreat. I called Daddy and asked him some questions. Mama had already passed away but for him the memories of their days together were as fresh as they had been seventy-four years earlier when they had begun that untraveled road together.

Here are some of my questions and Daddy's answers:

What Drew You to Mama?

Well, when I saw her, she was so pretty. I had no doubt that she was *the one*. I asked a friend her age. She was only fourteen, I was eighteen. I thought, *Oh, she is too young*. The next Sunday she was walking with the evangelist, I said, "If she is old enough to walk with the evangelist, she is old enough to walk with me." He said after that she walked with him until they were married, almost two years later.

What Did You Admire Most About Mama?

I told someone just today that I never heard my wife use bad language. She was always a good girl. There was never a hint she wanted to be bad. I admire her love for me, our family and her genuine Christianity.

What were some of the things you enjoyed doing together the most?

Everything. We did everything together. I helped her in the kitchen, because she needed the help and because I wanted to be near her. If she was able and wasn't needed in the house, she helped in the fields. I think it should be this way with a couple.

If there was anything you would do differently, what would it be?

I don't think anything. We had a good life. I don't know of anything I would change if I could.

If she was sitting here today what would be the
first words that you would say to her?

"I love you." He started crying on this one. I said, "Daddy, I'm sorry, I didn't mean to make you cry." He said, "Honey, it is okay, I'm just sentimental at this moment. A day doesn't go by that I don't miss her. I loved her so much."

What special thing did she do for you?

She always cooked what I liked. When we were first married, she knew I liked chocolate cake. She cooked a chocolate cake every week until I got to where I didn't care for it. She just tried to do what I liked. Anything she would find that I liked, she did it.

I then asked him what was some advice that he would give couples today. These are his words:

Balance. There must be balance. Each of you can't have your own way; you must be willing to give some, not if it's wrong of course. Marriage is a unit, work together. Don't expect too much from each other. A wife is not the underdog. God's word says for the husband to love his wife as Christ loved the church.

Trust each other. She didn't have to tell me every time she went into town, but she did. She always let me know where she was and what she would be doing. I didn't require this of her; she just did it because she wanted me to know.

Deal gently with each other. Before we were married, I told her to never call me a liar. I would never call her one. It just didn't sound good. I may tell something and not get all the facts just right; you can correct me when we get home. I have heard couples, one would be telling something and the other would say, "You're lying." Your mother was never a liar; it was always her intention, as well as mine, to tell things correctly. Deal gently with each other as a husband and wife. Never speak harsh words to each other. Words thrown out carelessly hurt. They may not have intended to hurt, but once spoken you can't undo them. You can ask forgiveness, but the word has gone out.

Mind the little things. Don't do the little things wrong. It's the little things that make people separate. The little things stir up wrath and grow into big things. Little things matter.

Tell your spouse you love them. Tell them with actions as well as words. Do say the words, but act like it also. *I was witness to this through the years. While Mama was in the hospital, I can't count the number of times I heard Daddy say, "You are my darling and I love you."*

Every day, you need to make this *day a good day.* Don't get too busy and drift apart. People separate because one of them gets too busy—too busy to show affection. Maintain your duty in every area of the marriage.

This conversation taught me many things. It taught me that I had to *work* at my marriage. It taught me that this oneness could be my greatest treasure on earth.

I watched as trials came into their lives, but Mama and Daddy showed us they could be overcome by facing them together in prayer with Godly guidance and counsel. They taught me there would be times of laughter, enjoy it to the fullest. They taught me my marriage could not only be successful, but it could flourish and bloom into beautiful.

Many years ago, I read an article that reminded me of my parents. It is a description of how I want my children to remember their mom and dad's marriage.

A Table for Two

To triumph in marriage means to have a partner—not someone who is always there, or always on target, or always anything. On the other hand, should I ever get into trouble and don't know who to look to for help; I can count on my partner.

Triumph in marriage is having someone to curl up with when the world seems cold and life uncertain. It is having someone that is as concerned as I am when our children are ill or facing tough times. It is having a hand that keeps checking my forehead when I'm not well.

Triumph is to have a shoulder to cry on as they lower your parents' body into the ground. It is wrapping wrinkled knees in warm blankets and giggling without teeth!

Triumph in marriage is saying, "When my time comes to leave this world and the chill of eternity blows away my birthdays and my future stands still in the night, it's your hand that I want to squeeze as I slip into eternity. And as the curtain closes on all I have attempted to do and be, I want to look into your eyes and see that I mattered. Not what I looked like. Not what I did or how much money I made. Not even how talented I was. I want to look into teary eyes of someone who loved me and see that I mattered" *(author unknown)*.

Johnny and I were flying to Idaho a few years ago and I struck up a conversation with the woman in the seat beside me. She had spent a month in Memphis with her daughter and her family.

We talked about our children and grandchildren. She told me her youngest daughter, who was twenty-four years old, and her new boyfriend were in Ecuador for a couple of weeks. She said, "This daughter is kind of a "free spirit," a new generation hippie. She has the piercings and tattoos, but they are dainty little flowers." She had told her mother that she would someday like to have children but was never getting married. The mom said, "I guess she has seen too much from her siblings." I had already asked her about her children, whether they were married. She had laughed and said, "Yes, I just wish they would stay married. All but one had been married and divorced twice."

Somewhere in the conversation she had told me she had been divorced three times. She had had two husbands and three divorces. She had married her first husband twice. We talked about the differences in our generation and our parents. How easily couples give up today.

After about thirty minutes of conversation I said, "Can I ask you something? If you don't want to answer just tell me that it is none of my business."

She said, "Sure." I asked her, "What do you attribute to the failure of your marriages?"

She replied, "Selfishness. There was the constant wanting our way regardless of the other's feelings. Not willing to give 100 percent of ourselves instead of the expected *fifty-fifty*." She talked a bit about how she had married young and her husband was verbally abusive, she had no self-esteem or self-worth. She said, "I am proud of my daughter I just visited. She is such a good wife and mother. She doesn't yell at the kids and doesn't have a bad mouth." She then said, "I have a bad mouth. I felt this was my only defense to the abuse from my husband. But I am working on this mouth."

There were four children married and divorced twice. One child was saying, "I will *never* get married!' and one was learning to change the pattern taught by her parents concerning marriage because she was determined to make a better life for herself and her family. I was saddened by our conversation. It was sad to hear the lessons she and her husbands had taught their children.

Mama and Daddy were young when they married; she was sixteen and he twenty. As with most marriages, theirs began with great expectation and dreams. Few of those dreams were realized. Most had to be set aside because life demanded attention and resources elsewhere. To them the words "for better, for worse" was a promise to uphold until death. They made an intentional choice to remain steadfast, faithful, and true to each other. The journey brought pleasure and grief, laughter and tears, triumph and disappointment, but they had committed for life. And they loved each other.

I'm thankful I was privileged to observe a long, loving marriage. I'm thankful Mama and Daddy made a life-long commitment. They were unwavering in their vows, "For better or for worse, richer or poorer, until death do us part." Theirs is a legacy I want to demonstrate in my own marriage. I want to see my children follow the same Godly example.

Thank you, Mama and Daddy, for showing me the meaning of true sacrifice. A marriage well done.

(1997/2013)

HONED BY LIFE
PART TWO

Just thinking…
about those hands-on experiences.

LESSONS LEARNED THROUGH HANDS-ON EXPERIENCE

*W*atching and doing is how we learn. Being who I am, I learn best and remember by the "touching and doing it myself."

Knowledge was gathered as I listened and watched; but most of the lessons learned on the farm were through active involvement and hands-on experience. Understanding has been acquired through the daily honing of life, listening to the preached Word and practical application. These valuable lessons have served as foundational principles to live by.

Make your day count. "Go to the ant…consider her ways and be wise." I've never seen a lazy ant. I have seen an ant carrying a load several times her size. As a science project I put ants in a jar with sand to observe their activity. The ant is constantly busy. She struggles with the burden of her load, but gets the job done. She also knows how to inspire her co-workers. It never fails to amaze me the things God uses to teach life lessons in Scripture.

Character matters. Godly character speaks for itself. The wise man's character is found in *"fearing God and keeping his commandments, for this is the whole of man"* (Ecclesiastes 12:13). The ruling factor of a person is found in Godly character.

Compromise forfeits God's resource for me.

Invite God into every area of life. "Behold, I stand at the door, and knock; if any man hear my voice, and open the door, I will come in to him, and will sup with him and he with me" (Revelations 3:20). God wants to be involved in my day-to-day life. He desires to have lunch with me daily!

Never buy into a lie. Error cloaked in truth will show up from time to time desiring you to embrace its teaching. Get so familiar with truth, the fake is easily and immediately recognized.

Busy is not always best. Notice this acronym:
Burdened
Under
Satan's
Yoke
I want fruitfulness, not busyness.

There is reward in trusting God. When we inspect the lives of the "heroes of faith" we find they were human, each had faults, yet those faults were not the focus in Scripture. What we find spotlighted for our example is their day by day living in faith. There was reward in faith. They obtained a good report. Their reward was God's approval.

Preparation for the challenges of the "unexpected" is prayer.

Most folk are followers; if you desire your world to change, be a leader in the right direction.

I find assurance in the Faithful God. *"The work of righteousness shall be peace, the effect of righteousness is quietness and assurance forever"* (Isaiah 32:17). Realizing God's faithfulness, I am assured my future has peace, faith, and hope—even when I don't understand his purpose.

It doesn't take a whole lot to be above average. It is found in the little things such as a kind word, a bit of attention, a card, a hug, or a smile. But it does require getting past our self-absorption.

Waiting gives strength and purpose. *"The LORD is good unto them that wait for him, to the soul that seeketh him. It is good that a man should both hope and quietly wait for the salvation of the LORD"* (Lamentations 3:25–26). The Lord is very unresponsive to an ultimatum. When we wait on the Lord for direction in life, we find strength and often saved from making wrong decisions.

Believe in someone. Bad choices happen. When mistakes occur, we each desire and need words of encouragement to try again. Believing in someone can make the difference between defeat and victory.

Children need responsibility. Responsibility brings blessings; the blessings include self-esteem and the feeling of belonging. Begin its teaching in the home at a young age.

Disagreement is inevitable. Having admirable social graces, great relationship principles, and valuable doctrinal truths will not keep us from encountering those that disagree with us.

> *"Let the words of my mouth and the meditation of my heart be acceptable to you, oh Lord."*
> *"A soft answer turneth away wrath: but grievous words stir up anger"* (Proverbs 15:1). How wise it is to think before I speak.

God is good all the time, his mercies offer a fresh start every day.
"It is of the LORD's mercies that we are not consumed, because his compassions fail not, They are new every morning; great is thy faithfulness. The LORD is my portion saith my soul; therefore will I hope in him" (Lamentations 3:22–24). Life doesn't always go as we dreamed and planned. But this I know, God has promised to walk beside me. In his presence I find fulness of joy. Not joy in my circumstance, but joy in his presence and goodness.

Laugh at yourself. I've learned to join in with those that laugh at my bloopers, slip-ups, and mistakes. I think there are times God must be sitting in heaven shaking his head, saying to Himself, "Did I really make this one?" Scripture says laughter is like a good medicine. Don't take yourself too seriously. Learn to laugh, it feels good.

Example: Many years ago, I was with my parents visiting a nearby church. I had gone to this church often through the years and had even been asked to sing. As I made my way to the platform that night, I felt embarrassed as everyone was staring at me a bit unusual. I sat beside the organ player and told her what I was going to sing. While I was sitting there, the pastor said (again), "I would like for *Sister Patton* to sing." I could have died! I thought the pastor had said for *Sis Padgett* to sing! No wonder I was getting unusual stares. The assistant pastor's wife, who was the organ player, told me everything was fine and to not be embarrassed. Well, thanks for those encouraging words, but I needed a hole in the floor, an exit door, some way to get out of the place. On top of this, earlier that day I had spilled hot grease on my foot; one foot was properly dressed in hose and shoe, the other properly bandaged at the emergency room. Talk about bringing the spotlight on myself! I have learned to laugh about this through the years. Why not? Nothing can be changed, except to listen more intently.

Example: I often keep a notepad near my bed to write down my *inspiring* thoughts during the night. One night I woke up with a song on my mind. I quickly jotted the words on my notepad. The next day my husband, his brother, and I were riding down the road and a song came on the radio. I said, "Wait a minute, I just wrote that song last night and it is already playing on the radio!" We have often laughed about this through the years. Thankfully not all my *in the night inspirations* and writing have this result.

My adventures are numerous and include ripping my dress apart at the city dump, landing on the restaurant floor when my husband pulled out my chair, and slamming my nose in the cabinet and the refrigerator (much to my family's amusement). I also need to mention almost jumping out of a van traveling at sixty miles per hour when an alligator tail flew out of a bucket and hit the roof, scaring me out the door. Too much time and space would be needed to tell of the incidents I can now laugh at concerning myself. Things weren't funny when they happened, but I quickly saw the hilarious in them and had a good laugh with everyone else. It is a good thing to smile, laugh, and enjoy life!

Our character must be tested and developed before we can realize the fulfillment of our dreams. It took Joseph many years to see his dreams fulfilled because God was working on his character. Development of character requires the process of tests and time.

Dreams will be challenged, and the anointing will be tested, but if the promise is from the Lord it will come to fruition...Just ask Joseph and David.

God first, then family. No one is as important as my family, *ever.* My husband, my forever life partner, the one to whom I've committed to walk this earthly journey, needs to know that he is the most important person in my life, without question. Forever and always.

"Our children are a heritage from the Lord. Love them, smother them with love. Some of the greatest gifts we can give our children are the assurance that we are encouragers of their dreams, wind beneath their wings and handfuls of hope in the darkest hours. We lift them when they fall, help them find balance and allow them to try again. If we want them to rest their feet on a solid foundation in their tomorrows, we must fill their lives with love, faith and compassion today." *(Author Unknown)*

Be sure to smile, laugh, hug and play, and do it every day. I love spending time and playing with my grandchildren. I have so much fun with those kiddos. They spoil me rotten! One day after I had spent some *silly time* with them, my daughter-in-law called and said, "I just have to tell you what Daniel said when he got home today. He said, 'Nana's cute,' but he meant Nana's funny." Another time I had pretended to be a mean, old lady and at their next visit they asked, "Nana, can we play, and you be the mean Nana?" Of course, I did.

Some of my favorite times with family is sitting together and telling crazy stories that have happened in our lives. I've learned it is the simple things, such as the laughter, the hugs, and playing with my family, that make lasting memories, bring us closer, and give opportunity to live life to its fullest.

Offer hope. I read somewhere that "faith is that secret ingredient that turns hopeless situations into salvageable ones, causing those that had no hope and thought there was no way to look for a way. There are days when most of us can be found caught somewhere between the painful memories and the terrifying present." *"If in this life only we have hope in Christ, we are of all men most miserable"* (1 Corinthians 15:19). As Christians, we have hope to offer, for this present life and the eternal. Give it freely.

Never throw a pity party.
Party 1: One day I was feeling a bit melancholy, downhearted, and lonely. I decided to take the trash to the dumpster. As I stepped out the back door I tripped and fell to the ground; the two large, black, full to the max, trash bags in each hand fell with me, ripping open and dumping trash all around me. I sat there in dismay, crying, a scratched leg and my pride hurt a good bit. Here I was on the ground, among the trash and not a soul in sight to help me. I finally said, "Eunice, get up, stop feeling sorry for yourself, pick up the mess, go get yourself cleaned up, and find something constructive to do." I obeyed, since the alternative wasn't going to be any fun.

Party 2: It was a troubling time and I was home alone while my family was at work. I felt like I was about to have a panic attack. I had to get outside. I sat on the back steps to have a good, screaming cry. As I sat down, I heard the church school kids having PE time next door. I *truly* wanted to scream then. I couldn't even have a decent pity party. I think the Lord planned it that I go talk and play with the children instead of having my little party.

Just Thinking, About Life

Maturity comes after a lot of living...
through mistakes,
through misunderstanding,
through hurt,
through loss,
through rejection,
through disappointment,
through responsibility,
through victories,
through love,
through living life.
one day at a time.

Don't ever run out of dreams. Dreaming is free, but there is a price to pay for the fulfillment of those dreams. Inconvenience, effort, and time are required when pursuing a dream.

I am responsible for my children. I cannot outsource this to anyone else.

My actions affect others. Most things I do in life touch someone in some way. My words, my actions and even my body language has some effect on those around me. I must remember someone is watching and following me. In whatever I do, I want to be found faithful and my life bring God glory.

When pursuing knowledge don't forget to allow wisdom to reign. There is a defining difference.

"There is a cure for 'stinkin thinkin,' it is to memorize and live" (Philippians 4:8). God's word never fails to give the proper insight and perspective to life. Reading Job chapter 38 will help.

Honor, Truth, and Integrity not only walk together they have voices of their own. *"He that walketh in his uprightness feareth the LORD; but he that is perverse in his ways despiseth him"* (Proverbs 14:2).

The voices of honor, truth and integrity will keep me pointed toward what God values. There is a consistent nudging toward uprightness even when it is unaccepted by many.

> *"The words of* wise men are heard in quiet
> *more than the cry of him that ruleth among fools."*
> (Ecclesiastes 9:17)

These voices are heard through a good conscience. *"For our rejoicing is this,* the testimony of a good conscience, *that in simplicity and godly sincerity, not with fleshly wisdom, but by the grace of God, we have had our conversation in the world, and more abundantly to you-ward."* (2 Corinthians 1:12)

The attributes of honesty, integrity, and ethics are a package deal.

Sometimes victories can only be celebrated for a moment. But be sure to celebrate!

The urgent is rarely the most important.

Don't let your dreams die. When your dreams die, you no longer believe in the dreams of others. *(Author Unknown)*

Those with a testimony have been tested. And survived!

Parenting isn't a popularity contest. There will be pleas from the child to compromise. If needed, turn a deaf ear. Always choose right.

Life...
Situations...
Frustrations...

Healing...
Help...
Finances...
Answers...
It comes down to one thing...
Trusting God to do what is *right*!

It is up to me how I respond to the hurt and disappointments of life. People have and will hurt me. There are times my own unwise decisions cause stress and discontent. I can use these times to grow or I can play the blame game.

Tough times have a way of bringing us to the point of total dependence upon God. Why do we not allow this to be a daily occurrence whether times be good or bad?

Life...

Through it all I learn...
To adjust...
To trust...
To be content....
All because of Jesus.

Presence is important. While cards, texts, and calls are appreciated, there are times that nothing compares to flesh and blood being present to share in my sorrow and joy. When someone is hurting, they need a heart that listens when no words are spoken. There is a need for a hand to hold as tears are shed. When achievements are met the joy is fuller when shared with those that care. I can't allow others to live life alone. Everyone needs someone.

New friends won't necessarily be true friends. It is important that I be cautious when inviting a new friendship into my life. What impact will the relationship have on the things most precious to me?

Seasons. They are a part of life. Seasons don't last forever whether it be a season of weather, a season of life or a season of a friendship. I've had to end a few friendships because their choices in life didn't align with the direction I wish to travel.

Lifelong friendships are priceless. I enjoy making new friends, but I want to make sure to keep the relationship of an old friend alive and thriving. Lifelong friendships are developed through the process of time and life events. These are rare and to be treasured. I don't want to do life without these lifelong, forever, until we die friends, or as one friend of mine said, "Until I pay off my Visa card!"

The true friend is with me in every season of life. This friend encourages as the heat of adversity tries to stifle any hope for life. She weeps when the bitter winds bring sorrow. She shares my joy in the refreshing rain of promise. We laugh together as life once again offers renewed hope. She stands in my defense and shouts the loudest in my victories. But she never hesitates to bring balance to the relationship with both rebuke and praise. This friend is worth the investment of my time, emotions, and resources.

The unrepented rebel will go on to perverse living.

We all get comfort and stability in routine. I must do my best to give it to my family.

Being wrong is difficult to admit. *"Therefore if thou bring thy gift to the altar, and there rememberest that thy brother hath ought against thee; Leave there thy gift before the altar and go thy way; first be reconciled to thy brother, and then come and offer thy gift"* (Matthew 5:23–24). Strength of character will allow me to eventually take ownership of my actions and say the needed words, "I was wrong." True repentance gives me the strength to walk the journey of consequence.

The real leader knows how to submit.

There is a difference between confidence and arrogance.

Opportunity and privilege are not the same.

Those things in which we allow God to work out in our lives will reflect his character and his likeness.

God is not slow concerning his promises. Most often I'm watching the wrong clock.

Desire has no strength outside of pursuit.

"I will bless the LORD at all times: his praise shall continually be in my mouth." (Psalm 34:1)

It never fails—we keep His Word; He keeps His promise. Yet we cannot expect the blessing without the responsibility.

True contentment comes from the Lord. Contentment and happiness are not always the same. Yet they are often found traveling together.

It is in Jesus that I live, I move and have my being…I cannot forget this. Not for one moment.

"Happy is that people whose God is the Lord."
(Psalm 144:15)

Jesus, to me he's become everything. All because he is God. In him I have a friend. He listens when I talk. He sees when I cry. He hears when I pray. There has never been and will never be a famine in his storehouse of answers to my prayer. And my situations never catch him by surprise.

I never outgrow the need for the voice of wisdom and integrity from my elders. When I begin to feel I have accomplished more than they I must stop and check my spirit. Then take time to sit and listen to tried wisdom. *"Remember the days of old, consider the years of many generations: ask thy father, and he will shew thee; thy elders and they will tell thee"* (Deuteronomy 32:7). We are instructed to favor the elders in our life lest we be judged.

Love is not a choice. It is a commandment. Choosing who and how is not an option. I'm instructed to love (Luke 10:27).

I cannot care for people more than they are willing to care for themselves.
Unfortunately, I am unable to help those not willing to help themselves. Whether it be spiritual, social, financial, diet, work, or play. Some things in life "they just gotta get for themselves."

Sometimes taking a step backward is not a bad thing.

The art of communication is often not saying a word.

It is the little things that bring big smiles and warm the heart.

Peer pressure can be an ugly thing.

If someone promises you the moon, don't accept—it isn't theirs to give.

It is unwise to become full of pride. No one is indispensable. There will always be a "new kid" on the block!

There is no such thing as independence. Everyone is always dependent upon something or someone.

The Golden Rule isn't "do good to me and I'll return the favor." It is "do good to them even if they respond negatively."

When my life is all about me, no one else matters.
When my life is about others, everyone matters.

Unfortunately, there are times the things we find intolerable in others is only a mirror to what we find in our own life.

Evil surmising: *"The needless thoughts that break relationships and end friendships."* If you aren't sure and need to know, ask (Philippians 4:8).

Allowing others to grow requires patience in me.

Unconditional love requires a lot of silence on my part.

The wise person will allow experience to teach by "watching" instead of "doing." These two—Been There and Done That—have testimonies that are worthy of our attention.

Pain and heartache would be my companion had God allowed me to always have what I thought best. God's "no" is to bless not harm.

My character has a reputation. As with Daniel facing his enemies, does the enemy of my soul know how I will respond to adversity? Is he aware that my faith is in God, not my own limited capabilities?

Trusting God quiets the anxiety, and faith is the refusal to panic.

Concern prays. Worry…well, it worries.

All things become beautiful when I trust God to do what is right.

It is the thankful prayer that calms the frenzy in my life.

This journey of life isn't all about me. I have others to consider. Jesus was asked, "What's the greatest of commandments?" His reply was, "The first is to love God and the second to love your neighbor." For my life to be blessed, I'm required to have a proper perspective for the divine and the human. When my focus is on God, I have assurance He can lift me above my circumstances. He is a big God; what seems overwhelming to me is but an opportunity for him to fashion me into his image. With proper focus and perspective, the good is discovered and things are better, not only for me, but for those around me.

Perspective defined is *a particular attitude toward or way of regarding something—point of view.*

Recently, while traveling I was once again reminded of how the landscape is so clear and distinct from a plane. There are defining borders scattered across the land. Homesteads are obvious by the tree lines, streams or garden plots. Rivers go in all direction as they wind through the lowland, fields are laid out in neat and precise order, and it seems the highest mountain can be touched.

Those things so large on the ground are tiny specks from the sky; semi-trucks look like Match Box cars, skyscrapers barely rise above the earth, and the lakes are but a puddle in the sand.

Flying high above my world, I see parking lots full of cars, the highways busy with traffic, representing thousands of people going here and there throughout the day.

As the darkness of evening approaches, there are multitudes of lights flickering in multitudes of houses, representing multitudes of people.

I have to ask, "Do these people know the great big God that meets my every need. Do they know He can take their cares upon His shoulders? Do they know Him as Savior?" I am reminded again; the harvest is great, and the laborers few. I have been instructed to "go" and help those around me discover the abundant life found in Jesus Christ.

My prayer is, "Lord, this life isn't all about me; show me the tool of the harvest. Teach me how to reach my world for You."

When I soar with Him, perspective changes, things look different and I hear my world's cry for help…*just thinking.*

For Future Generations

In the previous pages, I've shared my heart and many life lessons learned on the farm. I am grateful and thankful for the lessons I have been taught by my parents and through living life. They have become a part of my heritage. These principles are not my inheritance; they are a part of my heritage. There is a vast difference between inheritance and heritage. Inheritance comes easily. When a person dies, the heir is not required to do anything but accept what was left to him. It is something a person receives without any of his personal input and participation. Heritage and legacy are different than inheritance because they require one's active involvement.

I could define inheritance as a sum of money my father gives me at his death. An example of heritage would be a business that my father started, such as the home farm, but I must put my own blood, sweat, tears and prayer into it for it to yield crops and continue in business. Heritage calls for desire and passion. For it to develop into more than what it was when it was given to me, I must be willing to make any commitment and sacrifice.

While I have not chosen to live on the farm and continue the farm life of my parents, I have chosen to embrace the principles of life they taught. It is a legacy of which I am not ashamed, but grateful. I feel that all of life's lessons have been a heritage given me, worth much more than any "*thing.*" My desire and prayers are not only to live these lessons and principles before my own children and grandchildren, but that they will also embrace them as a heritage to build upon as they mature in life.

BLESSED
OF
GOD

GODLY PARENTS AND A
GIRL BLESSED OF GOD

I *am abundantly blessed, beyond words.*

Parents is defined as *the mother and father of a person.*

Good parenting defined: *the art and skill of raising children in the best way possible by providing their physical and emotional needs from infancy all through adulthood.*

My dictionary doesn't contain the words needed to express the love and appreciation I feel toward my parents. I haven't found the words needed to convey the Godly example and influence they both had in my life, but I try.

As an immature girl, *"Why?"* is the word that often came to my mind and out of my mouth when faced with their ideals, principles, and values. My parents never wavered from what they believed in and never veered from the convictions they held dear. Now that I'm older, with children and grandchildren of my own, I can appreciate their wisdom and the way they chose to live life. I'm so thankful for their gentle care and prayer that helped me over the bumps of life.

Mama worked long hours sewing to make sure I had something nice to wear, especially at Easter and Convention. Daddy worked many hours in the rain, the cold and in sickness so that I could have a new dress, shoes, or a school yearbook. Their parenting often required art, skill and sacrifice so that I might have my needs met, and some of the things I'd set my heart on having, and it was done in love.

Mama was our example in always honoring and respecting Daddy. He was the "king of the castle" and she was his queen. Daddy let us know Mama was the greatest woman in his world. Through this, I saw firsthand that two people can share a life and be happy and content.

I learned how to be a good wife to my husband through observing my mother's living example in the way she treated Daddy.

Mama was a good mother. She was upright, honest and faithful, responding to the challenges of motherhood with wisdom. The times I considered her unfair she continued to show me that true love is often tough love filled with a lot of hugs and prayer; and sometimes allowing me time to work through things on my own.

Daddy could have chosen any career, but I am so thankful my father obeyed God's call as a minister. He was diligent in teaching me the truths of the Bible. He didn't allow me to hang around with just any crowd, teaching me to choose my friends well. His calling had purpose.

God knew I would one day be the wife of a pastor and he was preparing me through the example of my mother. I've often heard her pray and weep over those in their pastorate. There were days it seemed so fruitless and hopeless, with little thanks. But herein was a valuable lesson; I needed to look past a person's failures and see the good that God sees.

The angels let us know there is great reward in seeing lost souls come to God, they rejoice in heaven. Mama showed me the importance of nourishing the lost soul, sharing tears with them in their mistakes, and then guiding them in ways to become victorious in Christ. Now that I share in my husband's ministry, I can better understand the fervent prayer and the sleepless nights. Yet words cannot describe the joy and satisfaction of seeing a life changed for Christ.

My parents both found God at a young age. They were both committed to God before marriage. They were dedicated to training each of us children in Truth and the principles of the Word. Nothing is greater than the Christian heritage that was passed on to me. I am thankful for Truth.

For almost fifty years, I have been blessed with a godly husband. Together we have borne two of the most wonderful children in the world. We have the responsibility to pass this wonderful doctrine of Truth to another generation. They have a great Christian heritage, on my parents' sides they are third generation Pentecost, on my husband's father's they are fourth, and on his mother's, they are fifth.

Even with this beautiful heritage, Greg and Melissa must search out answers for themselves. Thankfully, both have held fast to those things we feel that the Holy Scripture teaches. Not because of tradition and family, but because they have a personal relationship with Jesus Christ themselves. Our church and family are blessed to have them be a part.

Wednesday evening, February 11, 1998, Greg preached his first sermon. I was so proud and so thankful of his commitment to the cause of Christ. I wish my parents could have been there to share the moment. It was a part of them, a part of the heritage that they put into me years ago, something of which they could truly have been proud and thankful.

A while back, my pastor/husband had all the first-generation Pentecost come forward after he had preached. There were at least fifty people that came to the front. It was amazing. Not only did my parents influence my life, they also had impact in my husband's. My father was his pastor for several years. They were honored to have him in their life. And I am thankful for their Godly impact in his life, which has influenced our local assembly. Our lives really do affect more than us!

Realizing My Blessing

The root of stability, bringing strength into our home was Mama and Daddy staying in the Word. Both of their Bibles could usually be found on the kitchen table. Daddy always had a scrap of paper and pencil handy to jot down a thought as he read from God's holy script. There are the countless times I've seen Mama her in the rocking chair or at the table, Bible in her hands, with the covers folded back, reading from God's Word. They not only read the Word but were living example of the principles taught in the scripture.

As I have grown older, life has made me aware of the sacrifices they made for me. She worked when she was so sick. She pushed a chair around so she could walk when her back was so bad yet making sure the things the family needed were done. There were the long hours of working in the garden, putting up vegetables, sewing clothes, and working so hard with so little—no washing machine, no clothes dryer, no running water, no indoor plumbing, not enough heat in the winter, and no cooling in the summer. Yet we never went dirty and hungry nor did we burn up or freeze to death. When did she ever sleep? I don't think she did some nights.

I remember the many nights she got up to massage my legs when they were cramping so much due to "growing pain." When I was diagnosed with enlarged intestines, she would rub my stomach and worry about me (and pray). Yet she taught me God was a healer. He did heal me of that disease. Because of that healing I learned to trust Him for other healings and needs in my life.

She always put Daddy and us kids first. Many years down the road I realized the "pully bone" of the chicken wasn't really her favorite piece. It was chosen because it was the smallest, leaving the larger pieces for the rest of the family.

In my eyes, Daddy was a "one of a kind" type of man. He offered protection, support, and laughter. My earliest memories are of him reading to me and us lying on our backs in the front yard, watching the clouds form during the day or the stars at night. He knew spending time together was important to him and to me.

There are precious memories of the "storytelling" around the kitchen table. If that kitchen table could talk it would tell you of the many times I received correction, instruction in righteousness and guidance for a life to be lived in Godliness. It would tell you the "whys" I could not do certain things, such as date a particular boy and involve myself in certain activities. If you listened close enough, you would hear the laughter of a family enjoying a meal and talking about their day. With all those children and many guests there was much to tell. That table would tell you about family history, the joys and heartaches that have brought us to where we are today.

I tell about "the table" because that is where we spent so much time. That is where we ate, did our homework, read the Bible, shelled peas, cut out dresses, and talked with Mama as she cooked in the kitchen. The "table" was the center piece of our home. This is where Daddy was the head of the house. This is where I could get those words of advice I so needed, whether they were wanted or not.

There are no words for the gift of life lessons I've received from my parents. The blessings gained by intertwining them into my daily life, are too numerous to mention. Saying "I love you" is insufficient. The words "Thank you" inadequate. The only way I can effectively express my love and appreciation for their teaching and upbringing is by continuing to apply these lessons to my own life. Through this, perhaps I can influence the next generations with the same principles of living life to its fullest. I am blessed beyond measure.

THE FARMER
THE PREACHER,
THE PRODIGAL

THE FARMER

*H*e wasn't always a farmer, this father of mine. The year I was born he was a woodsman, a logger. I remember being told the story of how my daddy was injured trying, without success, to save his father from a falling tree. The doctors told Daddy the day he stopped moving, would be the day he stopped moving. My daddy has remained active every day, although *every* day was full of pain.

It was after the accident that my father purchased his in-law's property, a plot of 156 acres. This was the beginning of The Farmer that I would know and love. One hundred and fifty-six acres is a lot of garden plots. I don't ever remember not having a garden, and they were never a small garden. Whatever the season in Northwest Florida, my daddy had something growing. We seldom had flower gardens. Daddy's gardens weren't for beauty, they were always planted to provide food for the family, friends, half of the county and some folks in South Florida.

The Farmer's boots would hit the floor about three minutes before daylight. For a long time, I could never understand why he had to drop those boots to the floor every morning. Didn't he know we were asleep? Years later it dawned on me (no pun intended) that he *wanted* us to be awake, time was "a wasting." The Farmer did not tolerate laziness; if the sun was shining it was time to be moving!

The Farmer was old; I know this because he allowed me to pull out his grey hair when I was very, very young. He was old and bossy! He wanted us up making the beds, helping with the dishes and dressed for the field, all *before* sunup, or so it seemed back then. Truly, he did want us to be ready to get out to the field before the sun was up very long and the day became unbearably hot.

I make Daddy sound horrible, but he wasn't; he was a very loving father and a fun-loving man. I was just a child that wanted to play not labor in the fields. Daddy knew there was a lot of work to be done, the responsibilities were great and there was little time to accomplish the tasks within their timeframe. In his wisdom, he knew there was a time to plant and a time to harvest. Every season was important, and the work must be done at the right time or the farm could be lost.

The Farmer knew his seed. When I was young, he would save the current season's seed for the following year's planting. We had to take care of those seeds, lay them out to dry and then carefully put them inside a jar and place them in safekeeping for the next year. He knew they were good seed and we might not be able to find them next year at the farmer's market.

Most years, The Farmer would choose to experiment with at least one crop. This field was called "new ground." Careful and intentional planning was vital because it had never been used for planting the seed; a harvest was yet to be experienced. The soil was good ground, but because it was "new ground," a good bit of time and labor was required to get it where the seed could grow. The ground was prepared for tilling weeks earlier than planting day, not with a tractor, *but by hand*. Trees were cut, roots had to be removed, and rocks broken into smaller portions to be discarded.

The wind blew cold, the rain pounded, the hail hit hard, and the sun beat hot. The Farmer understood the weather was not always on his side. The days it was too hot and too little rain the plants withered and died. Then, the storm would come, there would be too much rain. The plowed fields stood deep in water and it was too late to plant. If the seed had been planted, the great amounts of rain either prevented growth or caused mildew in the crop. The Farmer prayed. The God that spoke the world into existence and said, "Let there be light" was the same God to provide the amount of sunshine and rain needed for producing a worthy crop. The Farmer prepared, planted and prayed; understanding God gave the increase.

The Farmer worked long hours. He knew it was the sluggard that didn't plow because of the heat or cold. The Farmer knew to have a harvest he must be diligent in every season.

The Farmer chose to be happy. He wanted his family to be happy and content. No matter how long the day, how hot the sun or cold the wind, nor how weary and tired, The Farmer had a whistle or song coming from his lips. When we heard his tune in the distance, as he walked the long lane from the field to the house, we knew he was headed home. The Farmer was coming, and all would be right in our world.

Reflections on The Farmer and my Heart

Discussions about life on the farm with my father, revisiting the work, effort and energy required for a garden made me think of my heart. For my heart to bloom, like my daddy's garden, daily attention is needed and essential for proper growth.

The heart is the whole of who I am. This is where my emotions, feelings and thoughts are processed. It is here that my personality is developed.

The changes and challenges life bring can make my heart feel like that "new ground" at the farm. I am often unprepared for what some days offer. I don't always respond wisely, leaving the ground unattended for weeds to grow. I didn't plant the weeds, yet, there they are waving bravely in the breeze. An unguarded heart will be attacked by bitterness, anxiety, feelings of doubt, hopelessness, fear, and even anger leaving no opportunity for growth, development and fruit.

I remember having to hoe our family garden. If we caught the weeds early, we could usually pull them out with our hands. If not, we had to get the hoe and really give the ground "a going over." This was harder because thorns often left us with blisters on our hands and an ache in our backs. It is the same with my heart, a "heartweed" must be quickly removed to prevent scars and heartache.

Years ago, I had a vine grow among my hedge bushes. This was one tough vine. I knew it had to go because it was killing my plants. I dug deep and finally got it out of my hedge. Recently, I noticed that it was back. It could hide for a while because it blended so well with my hedge. I pulled and pulled but was unable to get it out. I finally got the truck and hooked a rope around the vine and got it out of the plant. My heart is so like this vine. I think I have taken care of attitudes, only to have them crop up again later in life. Like my troublesome vine, I must dig deep and remove the root to prevent their ability to bloom again.

I was attending a ministers and wives conference. The speaker had taught on the necessity and benefits of forgiveness. At the end of his message he gave time for personal response to the Word. I knelt at my pew and said, "Lord, I'm not upset with anyone, I don't know of anyone I need to forgive." Immediately a voice spoke to my heart, "How would you feel had the situation turned out differently?" The Lord knew I was completely aware of what situation he meant. My answer wasn't pretty. At that moment I realized I still had ugly feelings resulting from an incident that had taken place years ago. They were buried deep. But God was giving me opportunity to repent, uproot and dispose of feelings that would eventually cause me problems sometime in the future.

We always had to fertilize our garden at some point during the growing season. What an awful smell! Life is like this; it often hands us times that "stink." Yet fertilizer has purpose. It brings growth and tenderness to the plant if handled properly and applied according to the package directions. If we can handle adversity and unfortunate situations properly, according to God's Word, our hearts will be as he intended; obedient, useful, and tender.

Wild animals had a way of getting into the garden, requiring Daddy to take protective action. He would have his gun ready, put up a scarecrow, hang aluminum pans to wave in the breeze, or place an electric fence around the garden to guard the future food for his family. What was wrong with the deer, the raccoons, rabbits and even the tiny, little fox? I thought these were just cute animals and he should leave them alone. I had no problems with the snakes, coyotes, and the panthers being killed or chased away, but kill the cute ones, no way. He would remind us of the scripture about the "little foxes spoiling the vine." How like my heart's garden; it is the little things, those seeming so harmless, that I have difficulty removing from my life. Guarding the heart requires awareness, alertness, and proactive protection.

Whatever the season, there was always something growing on the farm. If it wasn't crop time, we had fruit trees to tend. During the winter months the fruit trees stood bare, groaning in the wind. In the season of pruning beauty was absent. No leaves meant no shade. No shade meant exposure. I am not exempt from God's pruning. In this season, I feel completely stripped of everything, left with nothing to offer physically or emotionally. I feel defenseless against the storms, the hurt and the pain. But soon the beauty and blessings of God will once again be apparent in my life. The weariness of winter has moved to the beauty of spring, bringing a season of new hope. God knows the seasons. God knows the produce. God knows the farmhand. It is through the changes and challenges of the seasons where I grow, develop and bear fruit.

Daddy was an experienced farmer and had spent much of his life learning the land. He also spent much time in the Word and always had a scripture or word of wisdom. He believed we needed the Word and prayer; the abundant life requires both. His instruction was to pray before we read the Word so we could understand and apply the Word. The heart needs these instructions if we are to have growth and enjoy a harvest.

Daddy was growing old. He had a garden until he was ninety-four. He knew if he had a garden, there was still much work to do. A garden was no longer essential, my mother had passed away, there were no children at home to feed and he had family that made sure his needs were met. The garden had purpose; he needed to stay active for health reasons and he enjoyed sharing the fruit of the garden with others.

My heart is no different. I must stay active in the Word and prayer. Proper care of attitudes will produce a heart capable of sharing my bounty of blessing with my family, friends, and community.

I was reminded of this in a pre-service prayer meeting. I was sitting on the floor praying and my grandson, Joel, who was three at the time, came and sat on my lap. He said, "Nana, will you pray for me?" As I began to pray, I was overwhelmed with the great responsibility I have in helping to shape his life. To plant the right seeds in this little boy's life the seeds of kindness, love, rightness, and Truth had to be blooming in my heart. His younger brother, Daniel, came over and wanted Nana to pray for him also. Again, my heart swelled, and tears fell from my eyes as I prayed for those dear boys. I had a fresh realization of my need to keep the garden of my heart in good shape because I was not living for myself. I could not allow weeds to grow and crush my spirit. I prayed, "God create in me a clean heart, renew in me a right spirit, help me to live in a way that these children will always want to come and sit on my lap and say, 'Nana, pray with me.'" I have two more grandchildren now, Gabriel and Anna, and I want all four of them to know, by God's grace, that Nana's heart garden is well tended.

I never grow too old to not have need of instruction. Not long before my daddy died, he told me, "Honey, it doesn't matter how long you have lived for the Lord, Satan never stops reaching for your soul until the day you die. And he tries in so many subtle ways." This one statement has reinforced the need for me to guard the "garden of my heart" more diligently than ever.

Daddy had us children learn memory verses at a very young age. The first verse that I remember learning to quote, besides "Jesus wept," was Philippians 4:8: "*Finally brethren whatsoever things are true, whatsoever things are honest, whatsoever things are just, whatsoever things are pure, whatsoever things are lovely, whatsoever things are of good report; if there be any virtue and if there be any praise, think on these things.*" I have often referred to this verse through the years. Daddy was wise in planting this seed deep into my heart and memory. Its application to life has allowed my heart's garden to grow and bloom and hopefully give beauty and joy to those around me.

The Bible instructs us to plow the fallow ground. If left unplowed, hardness comes. When the rain of the Word and Spirit fall, I will be unaffected. Yet when I allow my heart to be dug around and turned upside down there is hope for the seed to grow and produce the desired fruit.

My goal is to have a heart pleasing to God, productive in whatever season he places me. I desire to receive the eternal blessings that await me on the other side.

I'm thankful for The Farmer God placed in my life. I am grateful for each lesson from the farm that can be applied to my adult life and integrated into my spiritual journey.

> *"For whatsoever a man soweth, that shall he also reap. For he that soweth to the flesh shall of the flesh reap corruption; but he that soweth to the Spirit shall of the Spirit reap life everlasting."* (Galatians 6:7–8)

THE PREACHER

*M*y daddy was a preacher when I was born. He told me he had felt a "call" as a very young boy. He said while working in the field and singing a deep feeling came on him that he would one day preach the gospel. This was a gospel that he didn't even know about until he was in his teens. After receiving the Holy Ghost at the age of twenty he often taught Bible studies. For a while he taught Bible studies in five different towns a week. It wasn't until he was in his forties that he became an ordained minister, but the "preacher" was there before the ordination.

The preacher and his children face the challenges of relationship the same as any other parent and child. According to some in a congregation the pastor's kid is born saved. In the Adkison family this was not the case. We faced the struggle of finding ourselves and our places in life as all families do. My parents weren't exempt from the process of their children challenging their belief system, rebelling their God-given authority or accepting the rules of the home. They had reprieve from much stress and anxiety when we finally had an understanding and appreciation for our parents' beliefs, boundaries, and teaching. Having eight children, this didn't happen at once. Some were not compliant and eager to embrace the Christian lifestyle.

As a child, I enjoyed my daddy being a preacher. I enjoyed the times I could travel and spend time with him. I enjoyed the attention I received as the child of the guest minister. Then, the early teen years hit us head on. I began questioning the things Daddy stood for as a Christian. Why was I born into a preacher's family? Everybody else doesn't have to live this way! My school friends didn't have to live by these rules, why should I? I didn't like being different. I didn't like living in the "glass house." And questions, there was always questions. Why aren't you allowed to do this? Why do you dress that way? Questions from friends and teachers. I had friends, good friends, a couple were PKs too, but their parents allowed them to participate in activities my father prohibited. Although my classmates and I had good times, I always felt different. Looking back, it wasn't so much the lack of participation that had me resisting; it was the natural maturing process to push and shove at my parent's boundaries.

Then there was a time my resistance wasn't as obvious. I didn't openly attack everything my parents required, but inside I was still struggling. My attitude was *"so what if Daddy is always on top of what I am doing, where I am going and who I have for friends. That's fine. That's just what being a preacher's kid requires."* Later in life I learned this was what being a child requires.

I had developed a way to fit in with the church crowd yet blend with my friends at school; or so I thought. Unknowing to me, Daddy wasn't fooled. He knew. And he knew this was a dangerous time for me. So into the prayer closet he went. I should have known things would be "revealed" to Daddy. I had seen it happen with my older siblings. Why did I think I was exempt? The intercessory prayer was where I became exposed. I could swear, which I knew better than do, therefore I "declared" that my daddy had eyes in the back of his head. God told him things about me! Not fair!

It took some time, a bit more maturity and my submission to a Savior that never gave up loving, calling and drawing, for me to better understand my preacher father's caution, care, and watchfulness. It was because he saw the effect my choice of friends, activities and decisions would have for eternity. Today, I am grateful for his diligence in instructing me toward righteousness for life.

Like the Farmer, he knew the importance of not only the seed, but the ground. He knew he had the responsibility to prepare the soil, plant the seed and water it with tears, prayer, and instruction. Just as with his vegetable garden, the Preacher knew the things hindering my spiritual growth must be plucked out or chased away before there could be a harvest. The Word informed him he had to give an account for my soul. So my preacher father prayed as he searched the Word for direction. It was constantly in conversation, verses quoted,

Bible stories told. This was The Preacher's way of planting its' principles into my heart. He then spent much time in prayer, believing and expecting a full surrender to God. The Preacher continued in this approach until the day I married and left his home to begin a new life with my husband. I am forever thankful.

Marriage and having children of my own brought a new awareness of the sacrifice made for me by my preacher father. The responsibility of training and teaching eternal souls were now in my hands. In this, as most likely no other way, could I better understand the years my father prayed, wept, and disciplined through biblical and practical instruction. I am so blessed to have had a praying father. He played an enormous part in making an eternal difference in my soul.

THE PRODIGAL

*P*rodigal is a sad word, bringing all kinds of images to the mind. The word can cause fear to grip the heart, sometimes to the point of losing your breath. The thought of the eternal destination of an unrepentant soul can bring me to desperation and even sapping the strength to focus.

What does it take to make a prodigal? Leaving home? Spending all of one's parent's money? Committing crime? Living the low life? No, one can be a prodigal and never leave the house and family. I was this prodigal.

I never ran away from home. Well, I did one time. My mother enjoyed telling about this little escapade. I'll tell my story, which is very close to hers. One day I got mad, very mad, about something, I cannot remember the reason. I packed an old, beat-up suitcase and down the road I went. My mother wasn't too disturbed, because she saw the direction I took, which was toward my older brother's house. She also knew what was in the suitcase. I had tossed in a few clothes but mostly it contained books. I walked about halfway, which was about an eighth of a mile, and became so tired. Those books were heavy. I sat down on the suitcase and had a pity party. No parents or sibling came looking for me, no car stopped to see if I was okay, and no police came to my rescue. After a while I decided to go home, realizing running away was too much trouble.

To be a prodigal, the individual doesn't need to run away from home. It is the rebelling against any attempt made for authority in his life that produces the prodigal. A prodigal is not always quarrelsome and defiant. I loved my home and the security it offered, but I often pushed the rules set for the family. My parents had intentionally set boundaries and they were in place for various reasons. My brain worked overtime conceiving ways to get those fences moved or taken down. My parents in their wisdom were usually one step ahead of me and had no intention of budging an inch.

I never tried to smoke nor drink. I never had a boyfriend outside of church. I never ran with the wrong crowd. My friends at school, for the most part, were the good "Christian" kids. I did try to "cuss" one time. My brother, Buddy, said, "You can't even cuss right." I never tried it again. Although I refrained from these things, there was a desire to *fit in* hounding me.

You see, a preacher's kid had rules, lots of rules. We couldn't do anything! My dress had to be below my knees, and this was the day of the mini, miniskirt. I mean everyone wore miniskirts. Can you imagine how it makes a girl feel when she is the only student in the entire school in a dress that covers her knees? Of course, I wasn't the only one, but in my teenage mind this was how it felt. My remedy? Roll it up a bit. The thing is when I rolled it where it was short enough, not even mini, but enough to fit in with other students, my waist was bulky and huge.

And the hair—oh, my long hair was definitely not the *in* thing at my school. My remedy? Make a ponytail on top of my head, pull it around, pin it in place, curl the ends a bit and tada! It looked cut. Who was I fooling? My friends were constantly asking me to take it down, let it hang long. They would say, "Why don't you wear your hair down? I wish mine was long like yours." Yeah, right. If that was the truth, why am I the only girl in school with uncut hair? I wasn't.

The deep-rooted teaching of being good and doing what was right was an expected way of life in our home. It began to be taught the day we were born. I loved my parents and desired to please them. My parents were the conscience always whispering in my ear preventing me to enjoy those moments when I stepped away from the boundaries they had set.

But I had wings that needed to be tried. I remember one year, seventh or eighth grade, our school trip was to a movie. The cost was twenty-five cents. We were to ride the school bus to the local theater, watch the movie and return by bus to the school for dismissal. I managed to get the twenty-five cents from somewhere. The day of the outing the students lined up to board the bus. As I got near the bus my heart began to pound extra hard. *Oh no! My daddy is a bus driver, what if he is today's driver?* Sigh of relief, he wasn't. We went into the theater, sat down and the movie began. My thoughts weren't focused on the movie. My thoughts were, *What if Daddy is the driver back to the school?* I couldn't enjoy the movie. I cannot tell you the storyline of the movie. I cannot tell you the title of the movie. I can tell you that I never went to another movie. Daddy wasn't there when I came out of the theater, but I didn't need his presence, my conscience knew that our family did not go to movies. I learned a lesson that day. Daddy's teaching wouldn't allow me to enjoy the opportunity of a sin moment, not one bit.

Daddy taught against organized sports. I couldn't understand why it was such a "big deal." I had never been to a football game and longed to go. I was spending the night with some of my relatives. They knew I wanted to go to the game, so they arranged to take me (a fact that my parents probably never knew, and then again, they probably did). As I sat there enjoying the game, I was thinking, *"Okay, what's the deal, what's wrong with this?"* In a bit an older boy, who was a friend, sat down beside me and started acting "overly affectionate." Although I had known him most of my life, I did not feel one bit comfortable in his presence that evening. I jumped up, found my relatives and asked to be taken home. God allowed a very unpleasant thing to happen to show me I could get into serious trouble by not obeying my parents.

My sophomore year a friend was having a party and invited me. I wanted to go. The main reason being that the guy I had a huge crush on was going to be there. Again, a relative dropped me off and said what time he would return. Things were fun for a while, then it got dark, the music became louder, dancing began, and cigarettes were passed around. Praise God, there was no alcohol or drugs. Not all my friends participated in this, but I began to feel uncomfortable. I walked around the corner to go inside and there was the guy I thought so cute and friendly; he had a cigarette in his hand, his arms around a girl and they were kissing. I quickly went to the host and asked to use the phone and called to be taken home. I was ready to get out of there. I couldn't enjoy the party because in my mind I could see my parents praying; God telling them where I was and what I was doing. I could see my daddy picking me up instead of the person that had dropped me off at the party. I never went to another party that wasn't supervised by a Christian couple. My relatives never assisted me in this kind of thing again and I don't remember asking.

One day my sister-in-law was going to take her children to the fair. She stopped by our house to get my brother and me. As we were about to leave Daddy came out to the car and quietly said to me, "Honey, don't put those pants on when you get to the fair." I'm sure my mouth hung open! How did he *know* that I had slipped a pair of pants into my bag? I declare, parents really do have eyes in the back of their head! You see, Daddy taught us from Scripture that pants weren't to be worn by women; therefore, I was not supposed to have them. I cannot tell you where this seventh grader even got them, nor can I tell you how I was going to get by with wearing them at the fair. After all my sister-in-law was there and not going to allow us out of her sight. A rebellious prodigal will try a lot of things, but a prodigal's Godly parent won't budge an inch in their beliefs and instruction.

Even in the frustration of being restrained it was through these times I learned valuable lessons. The protective fences will be climbed, sin tried, and disappointment encountered, but the prayer of Godly parents somehow makes these moments of rebellion uncomfortable, preventing any lasting enjoyment.

All of us siblings tried the rules and pushed at the restraints Mama and Daddy had in place. I was among the two or three that were stronger willed. By embracing this character trait trouble followed me. I desired my view to be heard. I became frustrated when I was expected to be silent in a matter. My parents allowed me to speak up, but often, my timing was off, way off.

During these years, I was an avid note writer. When I would be upset with my brothers, sisters or parents I would *honor* them with a personal note. The notes to my siblings were okay, I didn't care what they thought. But my parents, that was a different story. I remember writing a note or letter to them and leaving it in a well-placed position, so it could be found. These notes and letters were usually written after being corrected for a wrongdoing and I was venting. I would go and do other things, which was usually the task that I had been reprimanded for not getting done earlier. It was only a few minutes later that I would be praying my parents wouldn't find the note, or at least not read it before I could destroy the thing. I'm thankful that my parents had enough love and good sense to know that I didn't mean most of what I had written to them in my youthful pursuit of flying without capable wings.

My sisters didn't like to share their things with me. One sister is nine years older and the other seven years older than I. Why would they not want to share with their little sister? I just wanted to use their dumb hair rollers to curl my hair, so I could look pretty. What's so wrong with that? But they said, "No, you cannot use our hair rollers." They had taken the bristles out of the rollers and put them aside. I said, "Fine, I'll use these." I got my hair rolled but when it came time to take them out the hair was so entwined in the bristles it wouldn't budge. Every try to remove the hair became worse. I finally went to my mother crying for help. Let me just say that she was not happy with this darling girl of hers. At first, my sisters thought it hilarious but once they saw the difficult struggle my mother was having it was no longer funny and they joined in to help. Mama and my sisters worked on getting the brushes out for a few hours.

Unable to leave, since my body was attached to my head which was attached to my hair, I endured correction and instruction on leaving other people's belongings alone for most of the time Mama worked on my hair. She had the girls throw the brushes away and bought me some hair rollers of my own; mainly because she never wanted that experience again.

Tough love is a word this generation doesn't want to accept. I am a product of tough love and it worked. My parents stood strong in their conviction for what they felt the word of God taught through biblical principles. I tried to go my own way, but thankfully I was usually stopped from participating in ungodly activities and conversation. Disobedience wasn't tolerated and discipline was quickly administered. Was it easy for them? No. Was it pleasant for me? No. Was it needed? Yes. Was I helped? Most definitely.

The Potter's wheel was uncomfortable as God and my parents shaped, molded, and prepared me for what was ahead. Disobedience and rejection were my answer to the teachings and circumstances that God was using to draw me into a relationship with him. My rebellion was forfeiting what He was trying to teach me and depriving me of true contentment.

Daddy wasn't a professional businessman like some of my friend's fathers. He was a pastor of a small country church, supplementing his income by working at a grocery store and selling produce grown on the farm. While my friends seemed to have "zippidy-doo-dah" days, we plodded along in life. But Daddy was intent and focused on his goal. He never wavered or veered from the morals, commitments and things he felt right and most important. But to my young mind those other families seemed to leave us far behind with their successes in the community.

Daddy just kept doing what was right for our family. The teaching of the Word and Godly principles continued to be a daily occurrence. Today I recognize Daddy's wisdom, the things I thought brought my friends pleasure have proven to be the cause of much heartache. Many of those families have broken apart and are unsuccessful in the things that matter most; God, family, friends, and contentment. I'm thankful my desire for my family and me are not the choices of lifestyle I thought I wanted back then. Mama and Daddy's teaching, prayers, and daily living impacted my life early enough for me to make different choices for myself than those of a lot of my friends. These decisions for good have prevented many scars I would now carry had I chosen differently. Daddy's staying focused on righteousness has proven him the winner in both life and death.

Daddy and every preacher that came to our church preached the same salvation message. As a young child I knew from the word of God that I must believe Christ died for me and wanted me as his child. I knew repentance of my sins, being born of water and the Spirit were a part of the salvation process.

I received the Holy Ghost, speaking in a language I had not been taught except by His Spirit. I received this glorious experience at a hot, July summer Youth Camp near Orlando, Florida, in 1967.

I cannot tell you the exact date, but I can tell you the place, preacher and describe the experience. I can still see it all in my mind today, standing in the aisle of that small, white church filled with young people. I was praising God with all my heart.

Yet having received this experience, I still wasn't committed to Christ. It wasn't until the summer between my junior and senior year of high school that I made up my mind to totally surrender my life to God. I became frustrated with being two people. It was tiring trying to remember what I was supposed to be with my church friends and how I was to act around my worldly associates. Surrendering to Jesus Christ not only changed but transformed my life. Now that I was committed and my mind was made up, living for God wasn't an everyday fight. The shine and sparkle of the things the world offered no longer enticed me. I learned to be comfortable and contented with who I was in my relationship with Christ. Joy became a part of my every day. The Prodigal had come home. The fatted calf was killed, the robe wrapped around me, and the celebration had begun. I was back where I belonged. Reprieve from worry and release from daily anxiety for my parents had finally come. We could rejoice together and enjoy the journey ahead. We knew there would be times of disappointment in choices and making mistakes a part of life, but we were now in this together with the same goal of making heaven our home. I now realized the true significance of repentance, water baptism in the name of Jesus Christ, and the infilling of the Holy Ghost. These were the working of atonement in my life. The work of the Holy Ghost could now produce the fruit of that same Spirit. I thank God for my imperfect, tough love, praying parents. They never gave up on me.

I have a beautiful tree in my front yard. It wasn't always beautiful, full of leaves offering shade on a hot summer day. At one time is was scraggly, ugly, and showed no indication of growing. We watched it for years as it struggled to stand tall, add limbs, and offer shade. Twenty-five years later, we walked into the yard and the tree had grown taller, added leaves and was beautiful. It seemed it had all taken place over night. Today, it is one of the most magnificent trees I have ever seen. Each time I stop and look at it I am reminded there is always hope. What looked hopeless, threatened to be cut down and cast away, now stands tall and testifies that time offers hope like nothing else. Never give up, all things and people become beautiful in God's time.

Looking back, I realize I wasn't all that different from my peers. The teacher's daughter didn't always make the best grades in class. The policeman's son wasn't the best behaved in the school. The football players and cheerleaders had to be disciplined at times. We were all trying our wings and rebelling at conforming to the "rules," whatever they may be at the time. I now understand it was a part of our development and transition from child to maturity, a process we each had to go through yet feeling alone in it all. The wise parents kept teaching and training, knowing the lessons would one day be embraced and bring the good life to their child.

My life is a product of being *homegrown* on the farm. Growing up on the farm taught me many valuable lessons. Farm life was daily and provided many opportunities for *life lessons* to become implemented through practical application.

After leaving the farm, these *life lessons* have become a heritage in which I can be proud to build upon. They have helped me better myself as a citizen of my community and a laborer in the King's work. Application through daily living *honed* these principles into the very fiber of my being. The word, *hone* means *to improve something with refinement; to bring something to a state of increased intensity, excellence, or completion, especially over a period of time.* Hopefully, there has been a bit of refinement and some increased intensity, yet I have much to learn and I have not arrived. I am still on the *whetstone* in this school called Life.

Life offers us choices all along the way. Troubles, anxieties, and the daily grind of life have a way of offering me the choice to become bitter. I also have the choice to allow God to sift and refine me as he sees fit, developing godly character as I become a better person.

I have so much to thank God for, so much in which to give Him praise. You see, He's been so good to me. When I look back at where I've been, where He brought me from to where He has taken me, I am amazed. I stand in awe of my Lord. I have found

Him to be faithful to His Word. I have learned that God gives, and He takes away, yet I remain blessed. I'm not finished, because He is not finished. I am a product in the making. There will always be trying times, but I have reason to be joyful. The circumstances may look helpless, but God reminds me to sing. In the darkest of times, His light shines ensuring I won't fall when taking the next step. My loving God never leaves me alone. He never forsakes. He has been with me through the toughest of times. I am confident that he will travel the rest of the journey. It is the accumulation of the day to day living that has caused me to say, "I am blessed." Of all women, I am most blessed.

(1998–2013)

CONCLUSION

"*O*nly one life, twill soon be past, only what's done for Christ will last." I have heard these words from my father's lips my entire life. There were two plaques hanging on the walls of our home with these words in plain view. My parents knew the possibility of taking this onetime gift of life and wasting it.

One of my daddy's favorite passages from Scripture is found in Ecclesiastes 12:13–14: "*Let us hear the conclusion of the whole matter: Fear God, and keep his commandments: for this is the whole duty of man. For God shall bring every work into judgment, with every secret thing, whether it be good, or whether it be evil.*"

This motto and these verses were the very heart of my parents' teaching, through daily living on the farm.

I'm given one chance to live my life. After everything is finished and my life draws to a close, and I draw my final breath, nothing else will have mattered except being prepared for an eternity with Jesus Christ.

Mama and Daddy taught us there is a heaven to gain and a hell to shun. They began teaching this to me before I could comprehend their words or understand their meaning.

I believe heaven is real. I heard Mama and Daddy talk about going there my entire life. I believe that one day I will rejoice with them around the Throne of God. Together we will celebrate The Living King throughout the eternal ages.

But until then, I will go on living, giving practical application to those homegrown lessons from the farm and allowing the daily whetstone of life to hone me into a vessel of honor. Beyond doubt, I am a woman blessed of God.

CPSIA information can be obtained
at www.ICGtesting.com
Printed in the USA
LVHW041221110820
662878LV00003B/302